Oil and Gas Law in Nigeria
simplified

Other titles

Adah, C. O., *Law of Evidence*
Fogam, P., *Law of Contract*
Fogam, P., *Sale of Goods*
Obilade, O., *Nigerian Legal System*
Obilade, O., *Jurisprudence*

Oil and Gas Law in Nigeria
simplified

Yinka Omorogbe

MALTHOUSE PRESS LTD
Lagos, Benin, Ibadan, Jos, Oxford

Malthouse Press Limited
8, Amore Street, Off Toyin Street, Ikeja,
P.O. Box 500, Ikeja, Lagos State, Nigeria.

Lagos, Benin, Ibadan, Jos, Oxford, Port-Harcourt, Zaria

First published 2003
ISBN 978 023 133 1

Dedication

To all my children and godchildren:

Osaze, Brigho, Orobosa, Isoken, Osasu, Osayanmo, Ohimai, and Eseosa.

Some of you might actually end up using this book!

Acknowledgements

This book is a product of my years of teaching at the Universities of Benin and Lagos. I have to first acknowledge the influence that all my students have had on me and on my perception and understanding of the course. I also acknowledge the help and suggestions from some of my students, after they had graduated and here I mention Kent Nnadozie who is always available when I need some advice and documents, and my very dear John Sampson (deceased) who assisted me with materials at various times before his untimely demise.

I follow a path that has been trodden before. I acknowledge with gratitude the great influence of Prof. M.A. Ajomo, the pioneer teacher of oil and gas law, on my academic career. I affectionately acknowledge my lecturer in Petroleum and Energy Law at the University of Ife, Dr. Kola Adeniji (deceased). He succeeded in imparting a love of the course to me, and even though he had died by then, my earliest lectures owe a lot to his unpublished manuscript.

I acknowledge my first Dean, Professor Itse Sagay, who made me the pioneer teacher of Petroleum and Energy Law at the University of Benin, and I thank God that I commenced my academic career under such a distinguished scholar and in a Faculty where one had no in-house publications to fall back on. I thank God for the camaraderie in the Faculty of Law, University of Benin, up until I left. Without my experience there, I would not have known that academics can exist together as a family. I specially acknowledge Mr. G. Etikerentse, the author of the first book on Nigerian oil and gas law, who gave guest lectures to my class and took my students and I on yearly excursions to Escravos, throughout my period in the University of Benin.

I acknowledge Professor Dafe Otobo, editorial adviser to my publishers, who first suggested that I should write this book. Without him, I might never have written this book, and certainly, not this soon.

I acknowledge the helpful pressure of my husband, Allan, who was relentless in spurring me on to complete this work. I thank God for a husband who is not intimidated by a wife with intellectual pursuits, and of course, for being the Author and Finisher of my life. However, by His Grace, I am the author of this book and all mistakes and omissions are clearly mine.

Preface

This book is primarily designed for any student of oil and gas law in a Nigerian institution. It will also be useful to professionals involved in any aspect relating to the oil and gas industry, to persons working in oil and gas or related industries, and to anyone interested in knowing about the laws and regulations governing this very important industry.

The book is intended to complement the existing texts and several articles on the various topics dealt with. However, this book covers a basic syllabus in oil and gas law, as taught by the author in the universities of Benin and Lagos. It also includes topical issues that should be of interest to the reader. The intent is to introduce the reader to basic underlying concepts, and to selected existing literature at the end of each chapter. The final chapter contains sample questions, and covers all the topics dealt with.

Yinka Omorogbe

Contents

Topic I

Introduction

Introduction

Before considering the laws and policies regulating the oil industry, it is important to first understand precisely what we are talking about. What precisely is petroleum, and what makes it such an important commodity? Where is it found, and how is it produced? These questions are addressed here, even as an overview of the international oil industry is presented.

Petroleum

Petroleum is a compound mainly composed of hydrogen and carbon, and is commonly called a hydrocarbon. It can exist in gaseous, liquid or solid form. When it is found as a solid, it is either coal, shale, tar sands or bitumen. In liquid form, it is referred to as crude oil. Hydrocarbons in gaseous form are known as natural gas. The most commonly known hydrocarbon is crude oil, which is also referred to by many as petroleum. However, strictly speaking, this term - petroleum - covers other types of hydrocarbons.

Wide variations of crude oil exist, ranging from light volatile liquids or gases that condense into liquids at atmospheric pressure, to heavy mixtures that have to be warmed before they can flow. Crude oils also differ in colour, from green or yellow to brown or black. Crude oils often contain a number of other chemicals such as sulphur. Even natural gas is often found with other gases such as nitrogen and carbon dioxide. These are known as impurities and they tend to affect the commercial values of the particular crude or natural gas. Thus, a crude oil with a lot of impurities (e.g. 7% sulphur content) is referred to as a "sour" crude, while one with comparatively little (e.g. 0.5%) is called a "sweet" crude.

The value of crude oil is also affected by its weight. Generally the lighter crudes are more highly valued than the heavier crudes. Normal chemistry measurements for liquids are taken using specific gravity. The commonly utilised method of assessment in the oil industry is the American Petroleum Institute (API) grading system which is also based on specific gravity. Each crude oil is graded in API degrees which rate the weight of the crude by comparison with that of water, which has an API grading of 10 degrees. Crudes which are lighter than water have higher (API) degrees. In fact, most crudes are much lighter than water. Those with API degrees of 40^0 to 45^0 are said to be very light. Crudes above 30^0 are considered as light, those between 22^0 to 30^0 are classified as medium, whilst those below 22^0 are referred to as heavy crudes. A crude oil below 10^0 is regarded as very heavy and currently the cost of production of such crudes, using available technology, is so high that they are not generally commercially produced in large quantities.

The importance of petroleum

Petroleum is an extremely versatile commodity with very many industrial uses. It's importance however, lies in the fact that crude oil and natural gas are the most important sources of energy in the world today. It is true to say that the use of petroleum as an energy source made the twentieth century what it was.

> Oil has been known and used by man for thousands of years. The first oil well is said to have been dug in Shush, Southern Iran in about 500 BC and the Chinese are believed to have drilled for oil and gas with bamboo tubes and bronze drill bits as early as the third century BC. Originally oil was collected from natural surface seepages and shallow pits, and for hundreds of years was used mainly for medicinal purposes, waterproofing, occasionally as a basic lubricant, and for lighting. It was used as asphalt in the buildings and pavements of ancient Babylon.[1]
>
> The first modern commercial drilling and production of oil is usually said to have begun in 1859 in the US, when Col. Edwin L. Drake sunk a well in Pennsylvania near some natural oil seepages. He was working for the Pennsylvania Rock Oil Company, which was interested in using oil for lighting. However, some authorities claim the first modern oil well was sunk in 1806 near Charlottesville in West Virginia.
>
> During the late 19th and early 20th centuries the oil industry concentrated on extracting kerosene from crude oil for lamps and stoves. Its use as a lubricant also began

[1] This section is largely taken from *Basic Oil Industry Information*, publishe by the OPEC Public Information Department.

to be developed at this time. However, more important was the development of crude oil as a boiler fuel which soon became competitive with other established energy forms, particularly with coal in locomotives and ships. By World War I advances in refining had extended its use as a fuel for car and aero engines. The large-scale conversion of navies and merchant fleets to oil from coal helped to provide oil with an important boost.

With this rapid advance, by the 1930s oil began to compete with coal as the chief energy source for the world's industries. World consumption of oil rose from about one million barrels a day (b/d) in 1915 to over five million barrels a day by 1940. However, it was in the post-World War II period of reconstruction and growth, ending in the 1960s, that oil overtook coal's predominant position in world energy consumption, with total oil production reaching over 20 million barrels a day.

Energy

The following quotes both describe and highlight the importance of energy:

> Energy is one of the most familiar concepts. People may talk of the energy of a lively child, of the sun, of the waves or of the wind. They recognise that energy is stored in a spinning flywheel, in the wound spring of a watch or in the plutonium core of an atomic bomb.
>
> William Blake said, 'energy is eternal delight'. The author of an academic work on thermodynamics cautiously ventured: 'Energy may be thought of as a capacity for doing work.' And Einstein pointed out what each of these has in common with the others. "And

> energy is matter. It is this last which enables it to be said that energy is everything, the ultimate, irreducible essence of the universe."[2]
>
> The gulf between a highly developed and a subsistence economy does not exist because the researcher examining samples of moon rock is an inherently superior human being to the hill shepherd. It depends almost entirely on the relative availability of energy within their two societies. Like some great hovercraft, industrial society is lifted and maintained above concern with elemental necessities of life by a prodigious expenditure. Without this energy supply, the sophisticated skills of the industrial world are merely a burden in the struggle for survival.[3]

Energy is basically what makes things function. Energy is the underlying factor behind every type of activity or action. For this reason, the future of any society is dependent on its ability to have access to the energy that it needs. The amount of energy a society uses or has at its disposal is also a function of its level of development. Therefore one finds that the energy consumption of any of the developed countries is several times more than that of the average developing country. It can safely be said that any country whose energy needs are not being met will have severe development problems.

Other sources of energy

Conventional or commercial energy sources are coal, oil, gas, hydro-electricity and nuclear. The traditional or non-

[2] Gerald Foley, *The Energy Question*, at p. 1
[3] Ibid., at p. 3

conventional sources include firewood, animal dung, and agricultural wastes. Non-conventional sources of energy are those which are got from reliable energy forms, e.g. solar, wind, wave energy or bio-mass.

The international oil industry

The international oil industry is unique, primarily because of the importance of oil to the world economy as the world's major energy source, and the physical state of petroleum. The importance of energy is dealt with in a preceding section.

The physical state of petroleum has fundamentally affected the evolution of the industry. The fact that petroleum was either gas or liquid meant that transportation had to be an integral concern of any producer as large-scale movement required specially designed installations. Solids, on the other hand, are easier to transport and can often be carried and/or stored with other materials. In early days, oil was carried in barrels, then in bulk containers, and later through pipelines and increasingly larger tankers. The physical state of oil and the fact that several million barrels daily are utilised by the average industrial state, makes long-term storage a problem. Other solid commodities can be stored with greater ease, to the extent that a stockpile of several years can be built up by any consuming state. Even with increased technology this remains difficult for oil or natural gas.[4] Therefore the producers remain important and a force to be reckoned with.

The two factors above have contributed towards the tendencies in the growth of large mega – companies, and

---

[4] There are large storage tanks and underground artificial reservoirs.

towards the horizontal and vertical integration of oil companies.

Integration

The oil industry is capital intensive, transportation is an integral part, and crude oil must be refined before its value can be realised. Therefore a company which is involved in production, transportation, refining and retail distribution is at a clear advantage. A company involved in all these stages, so that it is possible for a barrel to be produced and to never leave the hands of the company's subsidiaries until it is sold to the final consumer is said to be vertically integrated.

Horizontally integration comes about as a result of co-operative efforts between the oil companies. High costs and technical reasons sometimes make it economical for companies to jointly explore and produce, and to co-operate with each other. Thus, the oil industry was controlled by the major international oil companies, who often acted in concert, sometimes in ways regarded as detrimental by their host states.[5] These companies, some of which have merged today, are still the world's largest companies.

How oil was formed

This section and the rest are taken from *Basic Oil Industry Information*, published by OPEC.

---

[5] See Topic VIII.

While in certain parts of the world oil seeps to the surface through cracks in the earth's crust, or because of certain geological formations, it is usually found fairly deep in the ground and under considerable pressure. Crude oil is a complex mixture of hydrogen and carbon atoms that was formed millions of years ago in a process that begun with decomposing sea organisms. These tiny sea creatures, as they decayed, sank to the bottom of the sea to become trapped in layers of mud. Over millions of years these sedimentary layers turned into rock, often overlaid in later geological time with impervious or non-porous rock layers.

Potential oil-bearing rock formations can be found all over the world where former marine basins existed. Under favourable conditions crude oil is generated in these sedimentary strata in a complex reaction involving considerable heat, time and pressure, and other factors, including bacterial action. Under the pressure of surrounding strata the oil tends to be forced out of its sedimentary source rock, and to migrate upwards through porous rock layers until it is trapped by a layer of impervious rock through which it cannot pass. Here it collects in what are known as oil reservoirs, geological formations that allow the oil to collect in pockets. It remains trapped in porous rock structures, usually limestone or sandstone. Oil sometimes can escape to the surface where it evaporates, leaving behind deposits of a thick hydrocarbon residue known as bitumen. Crude oil is usually created at least 1.500 metres below the earth's surface. However, subsequent geological movement, and the ability of oil to move upwards through porous rock layers means that most of the world's reservoirs are found between 600 to 3,000 metres below ground, though natural gas reservoirs tend to be found much deeper. A typical reservoir contains oil, along with water and gas trapped within fine rock pores and under tremendous pressure from the surrounding rock layers. Because crude oil is found in rock, it is also called mineral oil or rock oil.

Gas is often found with oil and is formed in the same process, though it is believed from decayed vegetable matter in former marshy areas. Natural gas is a hydrocarbon in gas form, and can be found on its own in natural gas reservoirs. Hydrocarbons are also found in more solid forms in tar sands, shale oil and coal.

Refining

By itself crude oil in an unrefined form has little or no direct use. Its value as a commodity is only realized when its many different hydrocarbon components are separated out, broken down or combined with other chemicals in a refinery to provide products that can be marketed. A crude oil's value, therefore, is directly related to the yield of useful products each barrel will produce as it is passed through a refinery. As the basic elements of crude oil, hydrogen and carbon form the main input into a refinery, combining into thousands of useful compounds. Tens of thousands of different products can be derived from crude oil. What can be extracted economically from a crude oil varies according to its particular individual qualities, and the processing facilities of a particular refinery.

In general, crude oil, once refined, yields three basic grouping of products which are produced when it is broken down into cuts or fractions: gas and gasoline, middle distillates, and fuel oil and residue cuts.

The gas and gasoline cuts form the lighter products of a barrel. They come from the more valuable top end of the barrel, and are sometimes referred to as white products, providing domestic gases, aviation fuels, motor fuels and raw material, or feedstocks for the petrochemical industry. Naphtha, a vital refinery cut, is extracted from both the light and middle range of distillate cuts. It is important in further refinery processes, forming a basic feedstock for other products, particularly in the improvement of gasoline quality for car engines, and as feedstock for the petrochemical industry. The middle distillates refer to products from the middle of a hypothetical barrel of crude such as kerosene, and light gas oil, heating oil, diesel oils and waxes, as well as some lubrication oils.

The remainder of the barrel, its bottom end cuts, include the black or heavy products such as fuel oil for power stations, industrial boilers and ship furnaces, as well as asphalt or bitumen used for roads, waterproofing and roofing and roofing materials. This residue end of the barrel can also produce heavy lubricating oils and waxes.

The actual proportions of lights, medium and heavy fractions that exist naturally in a barrel vary enormously from one crude to another. For instance, light North African crudes from Algeria or the Libyan Jamahiriya have high yields of light and middle distillates, while heavy crudes may yield almost no light products, with heavy fuel oil and residue accounting for over 80 per cent of a barrel in certain cases.

In the early days of the industry, the first refining processes were developed to extract kerosene for lamps. The light products and residue were considered waste and usually burnt off. The first refining processes were developed to purify, stabilize and improve the quality of kerosene. Gradually, however, other uses were developed for those parts of the barrel previously thrown away. By World War I, gasoline began to be used in increasing quantities as a motor fuel for cars and trucks. This demand on the products from the lighter end of the barrel grew fast, particularly when a new market also developed from aviation fuel. Refining methods had to be constantly adapted and improved to meet the quality requirements and special needs of car and aircraft engine developments.

Since then, the general trend throughout refining has been to produce more products or cuts from each barrel of crude, and to process those products in different ways to meet the increasingly exacting standards of modern engines and industrial needs. Overall, demand for gasoline has rapidly expanded with its widespread use in transport and the boom in car ownership that began in the 1950s. Demand has also developed for gas oils and fuels for domestic central heating, and fuel oil for power generation, as well as for light distillates and other inputs, derived from crude oil, for the petrochemical industries

But while demand for products derived from the top end of the barrel, the lighter cuts, has steadily increased, new discoveries have resulted in finding heavier type crudes. Crude oils yielding greater proportions of valuable light products are, therefore, relatively scarce and at a premium in the market. Naturally occurring light products in crude oil are insufficient to meet demand and so refineries have had to introduce complicated processes to win ever-greater quantities of lighter products from the heavier ends of the barrel. If, for instance, its main market is gasoline, the refinery will concentrate on breaking down the component parts of a barrel of crude oil in such a way as to maximize gasoline products. More complex plant and processes are required to extract, where possible, gasoline from other fractions of a barrel. The gains made in light products from such processes will result in a desirable decrease in the proportion of heavier products that would otherwise be extracted from a barrel.

What a refinery extracts from a barrel of crude oil, how it divides the cuts it takes from a barrel, depends on its processing facilities and plant, known as its configuration which is built as far as possible to meet specific demands for particular markets. A refinery configuration is, therefore, influenced by the specific demands of a market. But this configuration is also affected by the availability and price of different types of crude oil. Most refineries are built to handle a mixture of blends of specific crude oils with particular properties. These are selected to fit in with the refinery's configuration, set to meet the requirement of its product output pattern which is directly geared to the market it serves.

Refineries themselves usually have a life-span of up to 20 years, but they are constantly being adapted and upgraded to remain viable and responsive to ever changing patterns of crude supply and product market demands. The trend is away from heavier products, such as fuel oils, which are now in competition with oil alternatives such as coal, and towards lighter products such as gasoline diesel and aviation fuels. As a result, refineries have been introducing increasingly complex and expensive processes to gain more and more lighter products from the heavier and residual ends of a barrel.

Refining processes are continually changing, and today cover a variety of complex operations that are constantly being evolved and developed.

Terms commonly used in the oil industry

This section lists and briefly explains terms that are commonly used in the industry and which one is likely to come across in the course of study.

API degrees: Specific gravity is normally used to measure weight. In the oil industry, crude oil is measured in API degrees. On the API scale water has been given a measure of 10o API. Crudes lighter than water are given higher degrees. Example: Arabian Light is 34o API. This means that it is more than 3 times lighter than water. Generally speaking, crudes above 40o API are said to be very light. Those above 30o API are considered light crudes whilst those between 22o - 30o as classified as medium. Heavy crudes are below 22% . A crude which is less than 10o API will sink in water because it is heavier than water. Currently such crudes are not regarded as economically viable.

Some crude oil quality indicators

API GRAVITY (DENSITY)	
ABOVE 50 degree	CONDENSATE
33 - 50 degrees	LIGHT CRUDE
24 - 33 degrees	MEDIUM CRUDE
Below 24 degrees	HEAVY CRUDE
SULPHUR CONTENT	
BELOW 0.5%	LOW SULPHUR
0.5% - 1.5%	MEDIUM SULPHUR
ABOVE 1.5%	HIGH SULPHUR

Sweet crude: Crude oil with a very low sulphur content, such as 0.5% or less. Sulphur is graded as an impurity.

Sour crude: Crude oil with a high sulphur content, e.g. 2.5% or more.

Primary reservoir drive; the initial natural pressure in the reservoir which normally provides the natural drive to force the oil up through the rock pores, to the well, to the surface. Primary energy brings out only about 20-30% of the reservoir oil.

Secondary recovery: Techniques used to recover as much as possible of the reservoir oil remaining after the primary drive has been dissipated. Secondary recovery techniques involve the re-injection of gas or water into the reservoir to maintain pressure. Through these techniques, half the oil may be recovered.

Enhanced oil recovery: Sophisticated technique used to extract as much of the remaining oil as possible. These technologies often involve heat, special chemicals and solvents, and are normally tailored to the particular circumstances of the reservoir in question.

Proved reserves: A proved reserve is one where the figures given for oil in place indicate the volumes of hydrocarbons in known underground reservoirs that are estimated with reasonable certainty to be recoverable under existing economic conditions.

Potential or probable reserves: These are less certain than proved reserves, and are based on information gained from well logging and interpretations of core samples. They can be referred to as broad estimates of oil and gas that still remain to be discovered bearing in mind favourable trends in geological formations. Roughly half of potential reserves are estimated to be come proven reserves.

Possible reserves: These figures are the most uncertain. They are based on broad theoretical estimations of what could exist in place. Possible reserves are oil not yet discovered but expected to be present based on likely favourable geological conditions or trends. One could say that they are highly educated but speculative guesses.

Suggested reading materials

OPEC, *Basic Oil Industry Information,* Vienna

Gerald Foley, *The Energy Question*, Penguin, London 1992, particularly the Introduction and Part Two.

Y. Omorogbe, *The Oil and Gas Industry: Exploration and Production Contracts,* Malthouse Press, 1997, Chapter 1, 'Fundamental Premises'.

Topic II

The Nigerian oil industry

A historical perspective

Ascertaining exactly what the Nigerian legal regime is can be quite confusing, principally because what is contained in the main legislative enactment represents only a partial picture of what the current situation is. For better understanding, it is probably best to first consider the history of the oil industry and its attendant laws.

Nigerian legislation on petroleum had existed for about a decade before exploration was first undertaken. The first piece of legislation was the Petroleum Ordinance of 1889, which was followed by the Mineral Regulation (Oil) Ordinance of 1907, both of which laid down a basic framework for the development of petroleum and its natural resources. By the law of 1907, it was stipulated, *inter alia*, that only British subjects or companies controlled by British subjects would be eligible to explore for oil resources. However the first company ever to undertake exploration in Nigeria was the German Bitumen Company, in 1908, around what is now known as Ondo State. This exploration effort was unsuccessful and the company terminated its operations following the outbreak of World War I. However, that general area is now well known for its extensive bitumen reserves and plans are underway for its commercial exploitation as at the time of writing. The next concession was given to Shell D'Arcy Petroleum Development Company in 1938. It was an oil exploration licence covering the entire mainland of Nigeria (375,000 square miles). In the absence of competition, Shell was able to leisurely explore and select choice acreage until 1962, by which time it retained 15,000 square miles of the original concession area.

In 1959, the sole concessionary rights were reviewed, and various rights were extended to other companies of various nationalities, such as Mobil, Gulf (now Chevron), Agip, Safrap (Elf), Teneco and Amoseas (Texaco/Chevron). However, due to its previous monopolistic position, Shell remains the largest producer of Nigeria oil. About eighty per cent of all existing concessions are held by Shell and half of Nigeria's oil is produced within these arrangements.

In 1969, the existing petroleum legislation was repealed by the Petroleum Act 1969. That Act and its attendant Petroleum (Drilling and Production) Regulations, laid down what continues to be the foundation of the legal framework for the regulation of the oil industry in Nigeria.

In 1971 was a critical year for the oil industry. In April of that year, the Nigerian National Oil Corporation (NNOC) was formed and, in July, Nigeria joined the Organisation of Petroleum Exporting Countries. Although the NNOC was formed before Nigeria joined OPEC, it appears that its formation was in response to OPEC resolutions and policy statements which showed that the existence of a state oil corporation was an essential prerequisite for state participation in the oil industry.[1] Negotiations for participation led to the first participation agreement being signed with Elf, in 1971. Under this agreement, the government acquired a 35% participation interest in the Elf concession. In 1973, 35% participation interests were acquired in the Shell-BP, Mobil and Gulf concessions. Over the years these interests have increased to the current level of sixty per cent in all the concessions[2] except Shell's. Government participation in the Shell concessions increased to eighty per cent as a result of the nationalisation of British Petroleum (BP) interests in 1979. Since then the government has reduced its interests in stages to the present level of 55 per cent, to accommodate the other Nigerian liquefied natural gas partners, Elf and Agip.

In early 1972 the government announced the assignment to NNOC of all areas in the country not covered by existing licences or leases, and also any concession areas presently being held by other oil companies which might be surrendered from time to time.

In July 1973, Nigeria announced that no more oil concessions would be granted to any companies, organisations, and/or individuals, and no further concession applications would be entertained, although NNOC was free to select others as contractors or partners in working its concessions. This policy statement made by the government was never translated into any legislation. Similarly, the various participations were not dealt with under legislation. Notwithstanding this, these two measures had a profound

---

1 See Terisa Turner, "Nigeria: Imperialism, oil and the Comprador State," in Nore and Turner (eds), *Oil and Class Struggle* (Zed Press, 1981) 209, 221. Also Y. Omorogbe, "The Legal Framework for the Production of Petroleum in Nigeria" Vol. 5, No. 4 *Journal of Energy & Natural Resources Law*, 272 at 277.

2 Yinka Omorogbe, *op.cit.*

effect on the current legal framework, and fundamentally changed it in some important respects.

In July 1977, the Nigerian National Petroleum Corporation (NNPC) was created, as the result of a merger between NNOC and the Federal Ministry of Mines and Power. By this time production had been consistently on the rise, peaking at 2.3 million barrels/day by 1979. Then came the oil glut of the 1980s. Prices plummeted and exploration was greatly reduced. To encourage interest in exploration and oil and gas investments, the government entered into the first memorandum of understanding (MOU) with the oil companies in 1986. The MOU guarantee a profit margin to the companies. A second MOU came into force in 1991. The third MOU was signed in August 2000.

Currently Nigeria's proven reserves are estimated to be in excess of 21 billion barrels and it is the world's sixth largest producer of oil.

Legislation governing the oil industry

Various laws directly regulate the Nigerian oil industry, e.g., the Oil Pipelines Act 1956, Petroleum Profits Tax Act 1959 and the various Associated Gas Reinjection Acts. Others, such as the Oil Terminal Dues Act and the Oil in Navigable Water Acts, greatly affect oil and gas production activities. Here, the main focus is on the Petroleum Act 1969 and the Petroleum (Drilling and Production) Regulations 1969, both of which form the foundation for petroleum production and development in Nigeria.

The Petroleum Act 1969

Under the Petroleum Act of 1969, the entire ownership and control of all petroleum in, under or upon any land in Nigeria is vested in the state. Furthermore, the Act states that only Nigerian citizens or companies incorporated in Nigeria may be granted the following rights:[3]

(a) a licence, to be known as an oil exploration licence, to explore for petroleum. This licence must not exceed twelve thousand nine hundred and fifty kilometres in area.[4]
(b) a licence, to be known as a prospecting licence, to prospect for petroleum. This licence must not exceed two thousand five hundred and ninety square kilometres in area.
(c) a lease, to be known as an oil mining lease, to search for, win, work, carry away and dispose of petroleum. The oil-mining lease can only be in respect of a maximum area of two hundred and ninety five square kilometres.

Oil exploration licence [5]

This licence expires on 31 December of the year within which the grant was made and therefore may not be longer in duration than one calendar year. The right granted is non-exclusive, and several persons may be issued with licences in

---

[3] S. 2 Petroleum Act 1969

[4] S. 2(1) Petroleum Act 1969; Reg 2(1) Petroleum (Drilling and Production) Regulations 1969

[5] Paras 1-3, Sch. 1, Petroleum Act 1969; also the definition of 'explore' in s. 14, Petroleum Act 1969

respect of the same area. The activities which the licensee has rights to conduct consist of "a preliminary search by surface, geological and geophysical methods, including aerial surveys but excluding drilling below 91.44 metres."

OELs are rarely given nowadays.

Oil prospecting licence[6]

This licence confers exclusive rights to explore and prospect for petroleum and is for a maximum initial term of five years. Like the OEL, the area applied for is expected to have boundaries of straight lines running in north to south and east to west directions.

Oil mining lease[7]

An oil-mining lease grants exclusive rights over the lease area, and also confers interests over petroleum discovered within the area covered by the lease.

An oil-mining lease may be granted to the holder of an oil prospecting license who has:

> (a) satisfied all the conditions imposed on the licence or otherwise imposed on him by this Act; and
> (b) discovered oil in commercial quantities."

---

[6] Paras 5-7, Sch. 1, Petroleum Act 1969; regs, 2(2), 10-13, Petroleum (Drilling and Production) Regulations 1969.

[7] Paras, 8-11, Sch. 1, Petroleum Act 1969.

A discovery in commercial quantities is defined to be production of at least 10,000 barrels per day of crude oil. The duration of an OML must not exceed twenty years, but it may be renewed.

Rights and powers of holders of oil prospecting licences and oil mining leases over the licence or leased area

Rights and powers in respect of areas covered by the particular grants are dealt with in part III of the Petroleum (Drilling and Production) Regulations. These rights are subject to the applicable laws and to the approval of the Director of the Department of Petroleum Resources, a department located in the Federal Ministry of Petroleum Resources.[8] They may be exercised directly by the licensee or lessee, or through agents. The licensee may:

(a) cut down and clear timber and undergrowth;
(b) make roads;
(c) appropriate and use water found, provided that this does not interfere with the water rights enjoyed by the communities within the relevant area;
(d) construct, bring, maintain, alter, operate, dismantle, remove:
  (i) industrial buildings and installations, including drilling platforms, engines, power plants, flow-

[8] The Department of Petroleum Resources may be regarded as the "appropriate government agency"; but see Topic VIII especially pp, 111-113.

lines, storage tanks, loading terminals, harbours, jetties, piers, moles; landing places and derricks;

(ii) means of communications, including telephone lines and wireless stations;

(iii) facilities for shipping and aircraft;

(iv) living accommodation and amenities for the employees and workmen of the licensee or lessee; and

(v) other buildings, installations, works, chattels and effects;

(e) dredge; and

(f) search for, dig and get free of charge gravel, sand, clay and stone not subject to any licence or lease within unoccupied state land. This is on condition that it shall not be sold, and that upon termination or completion of work, all excavations shall be filled or levelled out, and restored as far as is practicable, to the original position.

The Act and Regulations make mention only of these licences or leases and not of other contractual rights. Therefore, it is only logical to presume that these are the only oil and gas rights in existence and available, even now. This is certainly not so. Participation has greatly affected the concessionary system, and led to the creation of joint ventures. Furthermore, there are other contractual forms such as the production sharing contract and the risk service contract which until recently, were not mentioned at all in any laws but which co-exist with these joint ventures.

Petroleum (Drilling and Production) Regulations 1969

These regulations were made in pursuance of powers conferred upon the Minister by Article 9 of the Petroleum Act, and deal with diverse matters such as the form and method of application for prospective licensees and lessees, and also rights and powers of licence and lease holders which have been discussed earlier. In addition, the Petroleum (Drilling and Production) Regulations 1969 provide for the recruitment and training of Nigerians, in pursuance of which lessees are required to submit a detailed programme. There is also an obligation not to pollute, or to "prevent the pollution of inland waters, rivers, water courses, the territorial waters of Nigeria or the high seas by oil, mud or other fluids or substances which might contaminate the water, banks or shore line, or which might cause harm or destruction to fish water or marine life, and where any such pollution occurs or has occurred, shall take prompt steps to control and, if possible, end it."[9]

Most of the regulations deal with technical matters and with the licensee's or lessee's conduct of operations. They provide that fields should be developed in strict accordance with a field development programme to be submitted to the Director of the Department of Petroleum Resources. Wells should be spaced. If technical considerations so dictate, an oil field should be developed as a unit. Records and reports

4. See section 2 (2), Petroleum Act 1969
5. Reg. 2 (2) P (D+P) Reg.
6. *Supra.*
7. *Supra.*
8. On OELs, OPLs, and OMLs see G. Etikerentse, *Nigeria Petroleum Law* (Macmillan, London, 1985) from p. 25.
9. Reg. 25.

should be maintained and from time to time forwarded to the Director. Fees, rents and royalties are also specified.

Since inception the Act and Regulations have remained the same except for some significant amendments such as the Marginal Fields Decree of 1996, and the Deep Offshore and Inland Basin Production Sharing Decree of 1999, which will be dealt with under a later topic.[10]

Other legislation

Several other laws are directly concerned with the oil and gas industry. Some, such as the Associated Gas Re-injection Decrees, the Petroleum Profits Tax Act, The Oil in Navigable Waters Act, and Oil Terminal Dues Act will be dealt with under the appropriate topics.

Some facts about the Nigerian oil industry

Nigerian crudes and condensate

	Crude oil grade	API degree
1.	Bonny Light	35.0
2.	Qua Iboe Light	36.0
3.	Escravos Light	36.0
4.	Brass Blend	43.0
5.	Pennington Light	36.0
6.	Forcados Blend	30.0
7.	Bonny Medium	26.5

[10] Under topic XIII.

8	Antan Blend	32.5
9.	Odudu Blend	28.5
10.	Oso Condensate	47.5

Oil terminal operations

There are two zones of terminal operations in Nigeria, they are:

Eastern Zone with five terminals: Bonny, Qua Iboe, Brass, Antan and Odudu (also known as Bonny) with the centre of co-ordination of activities at Port Harcourt.

Western Zone with three terminals: Forcados, Escravos and Pennington with the co-ordination centre at Warri.

The terminals have different storage capacities as follows:

- Bonny is the largest with a capacity of about 7.7 million barrels of crude oil, reduced to about 6.0 million barrels because some tanks are not in use.
- Forcados comprises 10 storage tanks with a capacity of about 4.2 million barrels.
- Escravos has 12 storage tanks with about 3.6m bbl
- Qua Iboe has a capacity for about 5 million bbl and
- Pennington has a stationary storage tank for 1.5 million bbls.

Source: M.M. Ibrahim, Lectures for Understanding the Oil and Gas Industry, Workshop organised by the Centre for Petroleum Environment and Development Studies (CEPEDS) May 1997, Lagos, Nigeria.

Crude oil/product supply and distribution in Nigeria

Refineries

There are four refineries in Nigeria

	Refinery	*Installed capacity*
1.	Old Port Harcourt	210,000 BPSD
2.	New Port Harcourt	150,000 BPSD
3.	Warri	120,000 BPSD
4.	Kaduna	110,000 BPSD

Pipeline transportation

SYSTEM 2A

The Pipeline network originates from the Warri refinery and supplies products through Benin and Ore depots up to Mosimi. There is also a coastal loading facility at Warri.

SYSTEM 2B

This system comprises two arms:

- A marine receipt facility at Atlas Cove from which coastal receipts from Port Harcourt or Warri from or Import Vessels are made and pumped into the marine depot. It is at this point that Aviation Fuel (ATK) is moved to the Murtala Muhammed International Airport depot. Three other product lines: automotive gas oil (AG=) diesel, kerosene (DPK) and Petrol (Premium motor spirit) are pumped to Ejigbo satellite depot.

- The second arm originates from Mosimi, conveys products to Ibadan and discharges same at Ilorin.

SYSTEM 2C

System 2C is the crude oil pipeline from Warri to Kaduna. The crude oil grades which utilise this pipeline are usually the imported Venezuelan crudes which give a higher yield of lubricating base oils.

SYSTEM 2D

This is the main pipeline network in the North. It originates from Kaduna and supplies products to 5 depots in Gusau, Kano, Maiduguri, Gombe and Jos.

SYSTEM 2E

This pipeline system covers the Eastern areas of the country. It originates from Port Harcourt and supplies Aba, Enugu, Calabar and Makurdi depots.

Coastal receipts

All loading made for Port Harcourt and Warri from the coast are supplied to Apapa and Atlas Cove jetties belonging to the marketers and NNPC respectively. There is a throughput arrangement with UNIPETROL that enables coastal receipts by creating an added logistic advantage of having two supply points in Ejigbo and Apapa area of Lagos.

Source: M.M. Ibrahim, *op.cit.*, Nigerian National Petroleum Corporation

Suggested reading materials

Y. Omorogbe, "The Legal Framework for the Production of Petroleum in Nigeria," Vol. 5, No. 4, *Journal of Energy and Natural Resources Law*, 273.

G. Etikerentse, *Nigerian Petroleum Law*, Macmillan Publishers, 1985, chap 1.

M. A. Ajomo, "Oil Law in Nigeria", in T.O. Elias (Ed.) *Law and Social Change in Nigeria*, University of Lagos and Evan Brothers Limited, 1972.

For stimulation, Terisa Turner "Nigeria: Imperialism Oil Technology and the Comprador State," in Petter Nore and Terisa Turner, *Oil and Class Struggle*, Zed Press 1981, Chapter 10.

Topic III

The ownership of oil and gas

This topic is concerned with ownership rights over oil and gas in situ. Ownership matters have been of great functional and symbolic significance in the oil industry world-wide, particularly during the 1960s and 1970s.

Traditionally, ownership is defined as the right of enjoying or disposing of a thing in the most absolute manner. In practice this right is often limited in some way or another. Thus Mr. X's right of ownership over his thing does not allow him to interfere with the ownership rights and rights of enjoyment that Mr. Y has over his own property. To give another example, if Mr. X should rent out his property to another person, Mr. X's ownership rights do not allow him to derogate from the various rights which his tenant possesses. Ownership is probably better described therefore as being composed of the following rights:[1]

- The power of enjoyment, to determine the use to which the thing is to be put, to deal with, produce, or to destroy it, as the owner pleases.

[1] See e.g. G. W. Paton, David P. Derham, *A Textbook of Jurisprudence*, Ch. XXI, S.115 at 517.

- The power of possession, which includes the right to exclude others.
- the power to alienate *inter vivos*.
- the power to bequeath by will.
- the power to charge as security.

An owner may grant to another person many or all his rights for a stipulated time period and still remain as owner. Therefore ownership has been regarded as a magnetic coil which remains when all present rights of ownership are removed from it, and which attracts to itself the various elements temporarily held by others as they lapse.

Ownership theories in the oil and gas industry[2]

There are various ownership theories. Here we consider:

1. Petroleum ownership under United States law.
2. The Domanial Law System.
3. Permanent sovereignty over natural resources and emergent international law.

Petroleum ownership under United States law

The oil industry originated in the United States of America. America was, and has remained the home of free enterprise. It is therefore not surprising that, unlike other parts of the world,

---

[2] Keith W. Blinn, Claude Duval, Honore le Leuch, Andre Pertuzzio, *International Petroleum Exploration and Exploitation Contracts*, Euromoney Publications, 1986, Ch. 1

there has been private ownership of mineral resources, including petroleum, right from the inception of the industry.

Ownership in the United States is conceptually different in another major respect. In certain jurisdictions ownership of oil *in situ* is not recognized, and ownership is said to occur only when the oil has been produced and reduced to possession. This position arose in the early days of the oil industry. Then there was little knowledge about the movement of petroleum underground. What was clearly evident was that it was capable of moving from under one piece of land to another. Thus in the *Barnard* case[3] in 1906, the court refused to enjoin drilling by an adjacent landowner alleged to be draining oil from a reservoir under the plaintiff's land, holding that the plaintiff's remedy was "self-help in drilling his own well."

In 1915 Texas courts adopted another ownership concept, reasoning that oil and gas beneath the earth belonged to the person who owned the land. Thus there are two broad ownership theories in the US today.

Qualified ownership theory

This theory obtains in states such as California and Indiana. Under this theory the landowner is said not to have title to the oil and gas in situ because of the fact that he can be divested by drainage without consent and without any liability on the part of the person causing the drainage.

However, he does have a property interest which is more than a right of capture. All the landowners over a common reservoir are designated as collective owners, with equal rights to take oil from the reservoir. The respective landowners do

---

[3] *Barnard* v *Monongahela Natural Gas Co.*, 216 Pa. 362, 65 A. 801 (1906), mentioned in Blinn, Duval, Le Leuch and Pertuzzio, *op. cit.* in note 2 above.

not have title to the specific oil and gas underneath their respective lands. They also do not have title as tenants in common to an undivided share of the oil and gas in the common reservoir which is equivalent to the amount of oil and gas under their respective lands. What each landowner has is an equal right with his co-land-owner to secure his proportionate part of the oil and gas in the common reservoir through wells drilled upon his land. He also has qualified title interest in the oil and gas as one of the collective owners.

Absolute ownership theory

This is found in Texas, Pennsylvania, Arkansas. The land-owner is regarded as having title in severalty to the oil and gas in place beneath his land. He is not a co-owner even when the reservoir straddles lands, each owned by a different person. However, he loses his title to an adjacent operator if the oil from his land migrates to the adjacent land and is produced from his neighbour's well. There is no cause of action for this divestiture of title by drainage.

Practically speaking the effects of the two theories are similar. In both theories the land-owner is not in fact entitled to oil and gas beneath his land. What he has are the rights to sink as many wells as he desires subject to good operating practices, and to extract as much oil and gas as he can produce.

The domanial system

The domanial law system provides for the vesting of ownership rights in the sovereign. This is the most prevalent system of ownership of minerals. Practically every country - with the major exception of the United States - retains sovereign rights over all mineral deposits. In a large number, this right is enshrined in their respective constitutions.

In Nigeria, according to the 1999 Constitution[4] the entire property in and control of all minerals, mineral oils and nature gas in, under or upon the territorial waters and the Exclusive Economic Zone of Nigeria shall vest in the Government of the Federation..." Also, under the Petroleum. Act 1969, the entire ownership and control of all petroleum in, under or upon any land is vested in the State.[5] The state then has the option of exploring and exploiting its natural resources by itself, or granting rights to third parties on whatever condition it may decide upon.

Permanent sovereignty over natural resources and emergent international law

The question of ownership over natural resources has received a lot of attention at international levels in the recent past. The trends shown reveal a shift away from investor ownership and control, towards state control and permanent sovereignty over natural resources.

In the latter part of the 19th century and the early part of the 20th century, the tendency was for the company charged with exploration and production of the natural resource in question, to exercise rights that amounted to sovereignty over the resource and the area in question. As the host countries became more aware they came to resent this state of affairs. In some instances there were nationalisations, as a result of which the nationalising state found that the investor company and its home state were insistent on international rules of

[4] Sec. 44(3) Constitution of the Federal Republic of Nigeria 1999.
[5] Sec. 1. Petroleum Act 1969

compensation. Invariably, these rules required the countries to pay out amounts far in excess of what they could afford, and which were often far more than they felt that the company in question merited.[6]

The developing and socialist countries attempted to redress what to them was an inequitable state of affairs, mainly through resolutions of the General Assembly.[7] On December 21, 1952 General Assembly Resolution No. 626 (VII) provided that:

> the right of peoples freely to use and exploit their natural wealth and resources is inherent in their sovereignty.

On December 14, 1962 the General Assembly adopted Resolution 1803 (XVII) titled 'Permanent Sovereignty over Natural Resources' which provided, *inter alia*, that:

> The right of peoples and nations to permanent sovereignty over their natural wealth and resources must be exercised in the interests of their national development and of the well-being of the people of the State concerned.

The resolution declared that:

> Nationalisation, expropriation or requisitioning shall be based on grounds or reasons of public utility, security or the national interest. In such cases the owner shall be paid appropriate compensation, in accordance with the rules in

---

[6] See Topic XIV below.

[7] Initial attempts to change the international legal status quo were made by the Latin Americans. This was through the insertion of clauses which placed the contracts within the ambit of national, and not international, law. This type of clause came to be known as the Calvo Clause after the jurist who was its major exponent.

> force in the State taking such measures and in accordance with international law.

The above statements were reinforced in 1966 by Resolution No. 2158 (XXI) which provided that the General Assembly should, amongst other things:

> Taking into account the fact that foreign capital, whether public or private, forthcoming at the request of the developing countries, can play an important role inasmuch as it supplements the efforts undertaken by them in the exploitation and development of their natural resources, provided that there is government supervision over the activity of foreign capital to ensure that it is used in the interest of national development:
>
> - Recognises the right of all countries, and in particular the developing countries, to secure and increase their share in the administration of enterprises which are fully or partly operated by foreign capital and have a greater share in the advantages and profits derived therefrom on an equitable basis, with due regard to development needs and objectives of the peoples concerned...
>
> - Considers that, when natural resources of the developing countries are exploited by foreign investors, the latter should undertake proper and accelerated training of national personnel at all levels and in all fields connected with such exploitation.

On December 12, 1974, the General Assembly adopted Resolution No. 3281 (XXIX), entitled "Charter of Economic Rights and Duties of States," which *inter alia*, stated the following:

> 1. Every State has and shall freely exercise full permanent sovereignty, including possession, use and

> disposal, over all of its wealth, natural resources and economic activities...
>
> 2. Each State has the right (c) to nationalize, expropriate or transfer ownership of foreign property in which case appropriate compensation shall be paid by the State adopting such measures, taking into account any relevant laws and regulations and all circumstances that the State considers pertinent. In any case where the question of compensation gives rise to a controversy, it shall be settled under the domestic law of the nationalizing State and by its Tribunals, unless it is freely and mutually agreed by all States concerned that other peaceful means be sought on the basis of the sovereign equality of States and in accordance with the principle of free choice of means.

These United Nations resolutions reveal a definite trend away from the traditional concepts of investor ownership - which emphasize the protection of individual rights - towards host state ownership of natural resources.

Selected reading materials

Keith W. Blinn, Claude Duval, Honore Le Leuch, Andre Pertuzzio. *International Petroleum Exploration and Exploitation Agreements: Legal, Economic and. Policy Aspects*, Euromoney Publication, 1986 at chapter 1.

J. E. S. Fawcett-Audrey Parry, *Law and International Resource Conflicts*, Clarendon Press 1981, 25 - 31.

Any international law textbook which deals with expropriation or/and nationalisation.

Topic IV

Contracts for exploration and production

Exploration and production contracts

A contract defines the legal obligations of two or more parties with respect to a particular venture or undertaking. In that sense, contracts for the exploration and production of crude oil are to be found in practically every country within which exploration and/or oil production takes place. Generally, these contracts operate within a legal regime that vests all mineral resources, including petroleum, in the state as sovereign.[1]

There are diverse types of contracts called by various names, and with many variations. Nonetheless, it is possible to classify all contracts under one of the following forms:

- the concession
- the production sharing contract
- the risk service contract
- the pure service contract
- the technical assistance agreement.

---

[1] The main exception to this being the United States, where mineral rights may be privately owned.

The concession

The concession may be subdivided into two groups - the traditional concession and the modern concession.

(a) The traditional concession

The earliest type of petroleum arrangement between governments and companies was the traditional concession. This was an agreement whereby the oil company received the exclusive right to explore for petroleum and, if petroleum was discovered, - to produce, market and transport the oil and gas. In return, the company paid some specified costs and taxes. These concessions had certain characteristics. First of all the contract area was often very large. In several instances, it extended over the whole of the national territory. Secondly, the duration was very long, typically between 40 years to 75 years.

The company was often granted extensive rights over all the mineral deposits in the area. It was exclusive owner and was free to dispose of them as it saw fit.

Financial benefits accruing to the host states were usually minimal. In many cases the companies paid a nominal rent of $150 and a bottle of rum for a whole concession. Royalties were based on volume of output, rather than value. For example, the Iraqi Agreement with the Khanaquin Oil Company in 1926 called for payment of four gold shillings per ton of crude oil produced and saved; the 1949 agreement between Saudi Arabia and Getty oil provided for royalty of US$0.50 per barrel.[2] No income tax was levied until 1950 when it was frequently set at a rate of 50 per cent.

---

[2] See David Smith, Louis T. Wells, "Mineral Agreements in Developing Countries: Structure and Substance" 69 AJIL 560.

These characteristic features were clearly inequitable and lopsided in favour of the oil companies, and therefore, such arrangements were unable to survive decolonisation and the new international economic order. The traditional concession is therefore generally regarded as a discredited form of contract, and the very word 'concession' has a bad connotation in many countries.

This prejudice stems more from the above main features which are peculiar to the traditional concession, than from the general characteristics of the contract type. In fact concessions thrive all over the world today in a modernised form and often with a different name (license, permit, lease or agreement).

(b) The modern concession

The definition of the modern concession remains the same. It is still an arrangement whereby the oil company receives the exclusive right, - in exchange for its payments of all costs and specified taxes, - to explore for petroleum and, if found, to produce, market and transport it. In other words, under this agreement the company has rights over the produced petroleum - it 'owns' it at the point of extraction. It is now called by various names e.g. license or lease, but it is still the most widely used type of agreement. In Nigeria what is known as an oil-mining lease, is by definition a concession. The terms which characterised the oil concession are now changed. The duration is normally for an initial period of twenty years. The area is greatly reduced, e.g. in Nigeria the maximum area for oil-mining leases under the Petroleum Regulations 1969 is 500 square miles.[3] The company is usually given rights only in respect of one mineral resource, crude oil, and sometimes,

[3] Sec. 2(2) Petroleum Act 1969.

natural gas. Financial obligations are greatly increased. Companies are liable to rents, royalties, and a higher tax rate which captures between 55 and 90 per cent of the economic rent on the average for the state. Petroleum in situ remains at all times the property of the state, in almost all agreements of this nature. However the contractor still has extensive rights over the petroleum, being granted the exclusive rights to explore search and drill for, produce, store, transport and sell petroleum found within the concession area.

As stated above Nigerian oil-mining leases are by definition, concessions. The oil-mining lease is specified in the Petroleum Act 1969, and is to be widely found in existence as one of the constituent agreements underlying the joint venture. It is much more rarely found existing by itself, being apparently reserved only for indigenous oil companies.

The production sharing contract

Production sharing contracts are legal arrangements in which the crude oil produced is shared by the parties in pre-determined proportions.[4] It originated in Indonesia where it was initially used for agricultural contracts. According to some sources it was first used for crude oil contracts in Iran. Since its inception it has provided extremely popular, and is extensively used in several countries all over the world.

In a standard PSC, the company bears all the risks of exploration, and is often in charge of the operation and management of the contract area. When oil is discovered in

[4] See Y. Omorogbe "Contractual Forms in the Oil Industry: The Nigerian Experience with Production Sharing Contracts" (1986) Vol. 20 *JWTL* (now *Journal of World Trade*) 342.

commercial quantities, the company is entitled to recoup its investments from the crude oil produced from the contract area. This portion of the oil is often referred to as cost recovery oil. Percentages of production set aside for cost recovery vary but are normally 40-50 per cent. The remaining production is shared between the parties. This sharing process is referred to as the production spilt. There is a wide variation in the ratios of production splits. They range from 81 to 90 per cent going to the NOC with a corresponding 19 to 10 per cent accruing to the private oil company in Egypt and Libya, to a 15 - 85 NOC/ company split in Chile. Invariably the party that is allocated a greater percentage of production is also the one that pays the rates and taxes. Therefore, in real terms the variations are not as striking as they seem. In a normal PSC, company income tax is paid, as the company is regarded as a contractor rather than an operator. The income tax rate assigned to the contractor might be borne by itself, or on its behalf by the NOC, as is the case in Egypt. However, in Nigeria petroleum profits tax is payable. Unlike the concession, ownership of petroleum discovered remains vested in the state or its NOC, and the contractor does not acquire title to its share of the petroleum until the oil reaches a mutually agreed point.

The risk service contract

Risk service contracts are arrangements whereby the contractor provides the entire risk capital for exploration and production. If no discovery is made the contract ceases to exist with no obligation on either party. In the event of a commercial discovery expenses are recouped and the contractor is entitled to payment, which is in cash, although often an option for payment to be made in crude oil is included within the contract. This method of payment constitutes the major difference between the risk service contract and the production sharing contract. As with the typical PSC,[5] the service contractor is normally subject to company income tax.

Risk service contracts have been extensively used in Brazil, Argentina, and Colombia, where a part of their appeal appears to lie in the fact that sovereignty over the resource is assured at all times. As is common with these countries, this sovereignty is often declared in no uncertain terms. However, their popularity has waned as a result of low oil prices and large debt burdens of developing countries. Thus, even these nationalistic Latin American countries have de-emphasized service contracts and have even entered into concessions.

The pure service contract

The pure service contract is a simple contract of work. All risks are borne by the state, and the contractor performs its stipulated services and is paid a flat fee for these services. Arrangements of this sort exist mainly in the oil-rich Middle East countries, e.g. Saudi Arabia, Kuwait, Qatar, Bahrain, Abu Dhabi. Often the service contract is accompanied by a legally unconnected but parallel purchase contract for part of the oil being produced from the contract area, as is the case in Saudi Arabia. It should be noted that the fact that the state is bearing all risks and costs does not imply a transfer of knowledge and/or technology, just as employing a contractor to build a house does not imply that the owner of a building will acquire

[5] In most other countries, not in Nigeria. See below pp. 53

any knowledge of the construction process as a result of the relationship.

Technical assistance agreements

Technical assistance agreements are of great significance for a country that is interested in developing a viable indigenous petroleum industry. On the face of it they are remarkably similar to pure service contracts, the main difference being that the company in question is engaged to provide technical services, without any interest in the oil at any time. However, technology and knowledge transfers are more likely to occur under this type of contract.

Under technical assistance agreements (TAA) the host country is exclusively responsible for the financing of the project. In addition, it owns the crude oil, equipment and facilities relating to the project, and manages it through the national oil company. The company provides technical services relating to all aspects of the project and seconds its own staff to run the project under the management of the national oil company. The company is purely a contractor without even purchase rights to any part of the production.

The technical assistance agreement has rightly been described as the most radical departure from the traditional corporation from owner to contract.[6] Currently only a few technical assistance agreements are to be found world-wide, in countries such as Iran and Venezuela.

---

[6] By S. K. B. Asante, "Restructuring Transnational Mineral Agreements", Vol. 73 *AJIL* 335

Participation and joint ventures

From the 1970s, it became increasingly common for host states to participate in their oil industries, not just as regulators, but as full-fledged partners in the enterprise. The result is that now participation by states is to be found in countries all over the world, the most notable exceptions being the United States and Great Britain. When the government participates, the resulting relationship is what is commonly known as a joint venture. When participation occurs, it is not uncommon for the foundational contract to remain in force. Thus, participation can be exercised with respect to an area being produced under a concession, a production sharing contract, or a service contract as the case may be. However, participation appears to be exercised most often in respect of concessions. The obvious reason for this is that participation (and partnership in the undertaking) can often be achieved through a judicious use of the inherent features of PSCs or risk service contracts. For a pure service contract, the question should not arise since by definition, the state owns the venture, and the company is operating as a contractor.

The relationship of participation is governed by other agreements, which co-exist with the foundational contract. These agreements define the relationships of the respective parties and usually they are the Participation Agreement, which sets out the respective interests of the parties in the concession; and the Operating Agreement which spells out the legal relationships between the owners of the leases and lays down the rules and procedures for joint development of the area and joint property.

It has already been stated that participation is an option exercised by the majority of states. However, as a result of the debt crisis and moves towards privatisation, it is currently experiencing a bit of a decline world-wide. In Nigeria, for example, the joint venture is the most important legal arrangement in the oil industry, and the great majority of crude oil is produced under it. However, there is currently a policy swing towards other options which are seen as being less expensive for the state to run. This view is buttressed by the fact that for the past few years, the state through the Nigeria National Petroleum Corporation (NNPC) has consistently been in arrears in making its joint venture payments. Whatever the outcome of the new policy shifts may be, and without going into the merits and demerits of the privatisation debate,[7] it should be borne in mind that participation remains a relevant concept. It articulates the ideals of self-reliance and economic independence that all progressive governments aspire to. Any shifts away from participation are more indicative of pragmatism than ideology and belief. Therefore the opinion here is that a positive change in the world economic climate, - particularly as concerns developing producers such as the Latin American countries and Nigeria - will lead to the re-emergence of state participation as a viable concept.

Legal relationships in the Nigerian oil industry

Currently, four types of legal arrangements for crude oil production exist in Nigeria. These are:

(1) the concession
(2) the joint venture
(3) the production sharing contract
(4) the service contract.

---

[7] Privatisation is discussed in Topic XIV below.

The concession

The concession is the oil-mining lease as stated under the Petroleum Act. Prior to participation, all the companies operated under this type of arrangement. Here the company fully bears all risks and costs of exploration, development and production, has interests over the crude oil produced and is liable for all royalty and petroleum profits tax payments. Currently concessions are awarded only to indigenous contractors. There are several such companies presently, some of which have become producers.[8]

The joint venture

When the government acquired participation interests in the concessions held by oil companies,[9] the new relationship that emerged was the joint venture.

Under the joint venture arrangements in Nigeria, the relationship is defined not only by the OML, but also by two other agreements:

(a) the participation agreement
(b) the operating agreement

The joint venture is also regulated by a third agreement, the Memorandum of Understanding (MOU).

The participation agreement

This agreement sets out the respective rights of partners to the joint venture. Such agreements vary in detail, because they

---

[8] See 'Indigenous Oil Companies' in Topic XIII below.

[9] Shell, Mobil, Gulf, Agip and Phillips, Elf, Texaco and Chevron and Pan Ocean.

were individually negotiated, but they remain the same in substance.

The interest paid for and acquired by the government through the Nigerian National Petroleum Company (NNPC) is referred to as a 'participating interest' in:

(i) the oil-mining lease;
(ii) the fixed and movable assets of the company in Nigeria, including without limitation, the company's exploration, development, production, transportation, storage, delivery and export operation and associated assets such as offices, housing and welfare facilities (the Assets).
(iii) the working capital applicable to the operation of the oil-mining leases, including without limitation, materials stocks including those in asset, debts of staff, debtors and repayment (the working capital).

The operating agreement

The operating agreement spells out the legal relationships between the owners of the respective leases, and lays down rules and procedures for the joint development of the area concerned, and of property jointly owned by the two parties.

Under these agreements 'joint property' practically all the activities and services of the oil company.[10] In all the agreements the private company is designated operator, and is responsible for the conduct of all joint venture operations. The operator may be changed in any one of the following circumstances:[11]

---

[10] M.M. Olisa, *Nigerian Petroleum Law and Practice*, 1997 at p.84
[11] Olisa, at 86 - 87.

(a) if the operator assigns or purports to assign its general powers and responsibilities and management, as operator of ongoing operations;
(b) if the operator ceases or threatens to cease to carry on its business or becomes bankrupt or insolvent or commits or suffers any act of bankruptcy or insolvency or makes any assignment for the benefit of creditors;
(c) If the operator defaults in its duties or obligation or any of them and fails to commence to rectify the default within thirty days after written notice from other co-venturers specifying the default; and
(d) In some cases; if the operator ceases to own, hold or represent a specified minimum percentage interest (usually 10%) in the venture.

The production sharing contract

In Nigeria, the PSC has had a chequered history. Like the service contract, the PSC was utilised by the Nigerian government as a response to the 1972 government policy shift away from concessions and towards contracts which emphasise the contractual status of the oil company. As a result the government entered into the first PSC, with Ashland Oil Company. Currently Ashland's interests in Nigeria have been assigned to Addax Petroleum.

The PSC (referred to as the Ashland PSC) was signed on 12 June 1973 for a term of 20 years, in respect of OPLs 48 and 98. This contract generated a lot of adverse criticism principally because of the way in which its fiscal terms were worded. According to these terms when a commercial discovery had been made, the costs were recoverable out of a maximum of 50 per cent per annum of the total crude oil produced. Of the balance, 55 per cent (slightly more than half) was allocated to Ashland as Tax Oil and the price received applied towards payment of Petroleum Profits Tax. Outstanding amounts payable as tax were borne by the two parties in proportion to their participating interest shares. The remaining crude oil, less than 25% of total production, was divided between the two parties. When production was less than 50,000 barrels a day the production split was 65/35 in Ashland's favour, and 70/30 when production exceeded this amount. On the face of it these clauses appeared lopsided in favour of the contractor. This was the opinion of the Tribunal of Enquiry set up to investigate an alleged loss of $2.8 billion from the accounts of NNPC, who felt that the PSC certainly has no benefits whatsoever to Nigeria.[12]

This PSC has undergone a few amendments, both formal and informal. For instance the Amendment Agreement of 1986 provides *inter alia*, for the provision and installation of a petroleum laboratory of a kind and cost acceptable to the parties in the Petroleum Training Institute, Warri. These costs are not to be chargeable as operating costs.

Current Nigerian PSCs

Between 1992 and 1993, having reached a consensus on the revised terms with the various Contractors, NNPC negotiated PSCs with Ashland Exploration, Mobil Producing, Elf, Agip, Statoil/BP, Esso and Shell Nigeria Exploration and Production

---

[12] Quoted in F. Sasegbon, "Current Development in Oil and Gas Law: Nigeria with comparative analysis with other African Oil Producing Countries" *Energy Law* Vol. 81; proceedings of a seminar organised by Committee on Energy and Natural Resources (Section on Business Law) International Bar Association, 361 at 371.

Company (SNEPCO). These PSCs span a period of 30 years (10 years exploration and 20 years production) with provisions for relinquishment of parts of the contract area.

The terms and conditions in the PSCs are substantially the same, with some modifications. Generally, they provide for tax oil in negotiated quantities to be allocated to NNPC for payment of "petroleum profit tax". However, these contracts appear to have a PPT rate of 50% indicated within their contracts. This rate, lower than what is contained in the PPTA, was recently given legal validity by s.3 (1), Deep Offshore and Inland Basin Production Sharing Contracts Decree 1999 which amended the PPT Act. Royalty oil is also allocated to NNPC for payment of royalty and concession rentals on behalf of itself and the Contractor. The volume of royalty oil is determined on the basis of the realisable price established by NNPC in respect of crude oil produced and lifted under the contract. Each contract is 'ring fenced, i.e. costs in one contract area cannot be deducted from revenues accruing from another area.

Cost oil is allocated to the contractor for the recovery of operating and capital costs. Operating costs are recovered in the year of expenditure while capital costs are recoverable in equal instalments over a five year period or over the remaining life of the contract, which ever is less.

The production splits vary from one PSC to another. For example, in the PSC dated 17 April, 1993 between NNPC and SNEPCO the following percentages apply:

Cumulative production from contract area (MMB)	**Profit oil NNPC**	**Percentages contractor**
0 – 350	20	80
351 – 750	35	65
751 – 1000	45	55
1001 – 1500	50	50

Cumulative production from contract area (MMB)	Profit oil NNPC	Percentages contractor
1501 – 2000	60	40

These figures are similar to the Esso PSCs.

In an NNPC/Statoil PSC, the profit-sharing ratio favours Statoil at lower production levels (up to 1000MMB cumulative production) over and above which profit is shared at a equal 50/50 proportion.

To control excessive spending by the contractor there are expenditure limits in excess of which the contract must seek NNPC's prior approval. For example, in the NNPC/Statoil PSC, the prior approval of NNPC must be obtained both in respect of foreign purchases exceeding \$100,000.00 and in respect of local purchases and contracts exceeding \$100,000.00.

Furthermore, work programmes and budgets are reviewed and approved by the management committee to ensure that operations are carried out in a proper and workmanlike manner.

Allocations of crude oil proceeds are in the priority order of royalty oil, cost oil, tax oil and profit oil, therefore, profit oil can only result where proceeds remain. Allocations are made on a monthly basis according to their previously negotiated proportions. Where the proceeds from tax oil, cost oil and royalty oil are insufficient to fully discharge their corresponding liabilities, the excess is carried over to the following month.

Each party is free to take in kind, lift and dispose of its allocation of available crude oil in accordance with the lifting procedure which is annexed to and made part of the PSC.

The service contract

The service contract is currently not very popular in Nigeria. There is only one existing service contract with Agip Energy as at the time of writing. The duration of the contract is initially expressed only in terms of an exploration period of 3 years plus one or two further renewal periods of two years. It automatically terminates after these periods if no discovery has been made. However, in the event of a commercial discovery, a contract term may be decided on by the parties.

Where an approved exploration programme does not lead to commercial discovery, fifty per cent of all exploration costs shall be reimbursed out of the proceeds of sales of production from the contract area. Also, if a commercial discovery is made in the contract area during the last five years of the contract term, NNPC and Contractor will meet and agree on terms which will enable the contractor to recover its costs and to earn adequate remuneration even beyond the contract term.

The contractor pays normal company income tax on its remuneration, while NNPC pays all petroleum profits tax and royalties. Within the contract, provision is also made for NNPC to take over and conduct all operations, although this provision does not yet appear to have been utilised.

Selected reading materials

M. M. Olisa, *Nigerian Petroleum Law and Practice*, 2nd Edition, Martin M. Olisa, 1997.

David N. Smith, Louis T. Wells, "Mineral Agreements in Developing Countries: Structures and Substance", 69 *AJIL* 560.

S. K. B. Asante, "Restructuring Transnational Mineral Agreements" 73 *AJIL* 335.

Y, Omorogbe, "Contractual Forms in the Oil Industry: the Nigerian Experience with Production Sharing Contracts," 1986, *Journal of World Trade,* Vol. 20, No. 3, 342.

Sola Adepetun - Yomi Audifferen, "Production-Sharing Contracts: the Nigerian Experience,' (1995) Vol. 13. Issue 2, *Oil and Gas and Taxation Review,* 73.

Y. Omorogbe, 'The Legal Regime for Petroleum Production and Development in Nigeria,' in C.O. Okonkwo (Ed), *Contemporary Issues in Nigerian Law: Essays in honour of Judge Bola Ajibola,* 1985.

Topic V

The natural gas industry

International natural gas market

The natural gas market is very different from that of crude oil, largely because of the different physical characteristics. While both are hydrocarbons and can be used interchangeably as energy sources and in several types of industries,[*] the infrastructure and long-term planning for natural gas is far more complex. Its natural gaseous state means that it can only be commercially transported in gaseous form via pipelines, or in liquefied form in specially constructed cryogenic tankers. Both these modes require definite buyers who will be linked to their sellers through the pipeline network, or who will have re-gasification plants to convert the liquefied natural gas (LNG) back to natural gas, as the case may be. Internationally, three major markets exist.[1] There is an Asian market consisting of Japan principally, and to a lesser extent Korea and Taiwan.

---

[*] See Gerald Greenwald, "Encouraging Natural Gas Exploration Policies," in Nicky Beredjick-Thomas Walde, *Petroleum Policies in Developing Countries*, Grahan & Trotman, 1988, 175 at 176.

[1] See "Lower Oil Price Starts to Dent Growth in Gas Trade," in *Petroleum Intelligence Weekly*, 11 April 1994 at p 5.

Secondly a European market exists which is linked by pipeline to natural gas imports from the Netherlands, the former Soviet Union, and Algeria, but which also currently takes LNG imports from Algeria and Libya. The United States is the third market, largely through imports from Canada and Mexico. The nature of gas makes the natural gas market largely inflexible, and it is difficult for new suppliers to enter into existing markets, particularly if the suppliers are situated some distance away from prospective markets. The market continues to be dominated by a few big sellers selling to a few big buyers and. this trend is unlikely to change.

The Nigerian market for natural gas

The alternative to the international market is the domestic market, and for developing countries generally this is fraught with problems, mainly because the commercial usage of natural gas within a domestic setting requires levels of technology, infrastructure and investment that are not normally found in developing countries, and which do not currently pertain in Nigeria.

Also the use of gas requires some knowledge and understanding and therefore care has to be taken if it is being used in a typical Third World rural setting. However gas is presently utilised to an extent, and it is being used increasingly in new schemes.

There are two main gas suppliers in Nigeria – the Nigerian Gas Company (NGC) and Shell Nigeria Gas Limited. A third company was GasLink, which was initially to cater for customers in the Ikeja industrial area. The major gas user is the National Electric Power Authority which pays a highly subsidised price for its gas. Some other customers include the National Fertiliser Corporation of

Nigeria (NAFCON), Michelin and West African Portland Cement. The customers for natural gas are located in the south and are mainly linked to the Escravos-Lagos pipeline. There is currently no pipeline network for the northern states.

There are some new projects in the pipeline. The older ones are responses to government incentives for gas utilisation, whilst the newer projects have been stimulated by the new liberalisation. As an example of the latter, the Lagos State government has initiated a gas turbine power plant, to improve the electricity supply of the state. The project is jointly owned by the Lagos State government, Enron Power Nigeria Limited and an indigenous company, Yinka Folawiyo Power Limited. An emergency supply of electricity was to commence in October 1999 and to be generated from a barge The plant is to be completed in approximately two years.

Natural gas contracts

Natural gas contracts reflect the nature and rigidity of international gas trade. The high investments required coupled with the physical state of gas mean that agreements are for long periods of typically 35-40 years. These factors also mean that, as far as possible, parties seek guarantees that their obligations will be met, failing which the aggrieved party will be entitled to damages. It is quite usual for sales agreements to be concluded before the natural gas facilities have been concluded. Thus, NLNG's buyers for the Nigerian Liquefied Natural Gas project were completely committed years before the first shipment was made.

In a typical gas sales agreement for a stipulated period of time, the parties agree on the price for the gas and the payment regime. There is always a take-or-pay clause under which the buyers agree to take minimum quantities of gas for the duration of the agreement. In the event of failure to take the stipulated amount he agrees to pay for the gas, up to a stated amount. This gas, which is paid for but not taken, is referred to as Make-up Gas and may be subsequently taken by the buyers, after he has taken his annual contract quantity (ACQ). The gas must be of the agreed contract quality.

Gas flaring in Nigeria

Gas flaring on a large scale is an extremely wasteful and environmentally harmful practice which is now universally discouraged as it is a major contributor of greenhouse gas (see Topic XI below). Nigeria has one of the world's worst flaring rates of about 70%.

In the 1970s the government recognised the potential of the natural gas industry, and for the first time, promulgated legislation banning gas flaring. According to the Associated Gas Reinjection Act 1979, all companies were to submit gas utilisation preliminary programmes by 1 April 1980, and detailed programmes on utilisation or reinjection by 1 January 1980. No company was to flare gas after 1 January 1984 without the permission of the Minister. The penalty for non-compliance in the original enactment was the stringent, if unrealistic, punishment of forfeiture of concessions.

The deadline was shifted twice, to 1 April 1984, and then to 1 January 1985. Finally, the Associated Gas Reinjection (Continued Flaring of Gas) Regulations 1984 came into force and provided for exemptions to the general ban on flaring. These clauses, according to the Petroleum Economist at the time, had the effect of exempting 55 out of 84 Shell fields, 10 out of Mobil's 15, 4 out of Agip's 22,7 out of Gulf's 17,3 out of Texaco's 5,4 out of Elf's 6,1 out of Ashland's 3, and 1 each for Tenneco and Pan Ocean. A total of 86 out of 155 fields thereby remained exempted from the anti-flaring provisions. The remaining fields were subject to a fairly insignificant penalty which made it far more economical for the companies to flare than to utilise or reinject gas. Thus Gulf Oil[2] stated that while gas flaring would cost the company $1 million, the costs of switching from water to gas injection would cost $56 million.[3]

The easing of the government position was as a result of various factors. First, the laws were promulgated despite the absence of any infrastructure for associated gas utilisation. At that time only one gas injection plant owned by Mobil existed. The LNG Project was stalled, and the Escravos-Lagos pipeline had not been completed. Secondly, there was the problem of finance. Since the bulk of Nigerian oil is produced under joint ventures where the government through NNPC is the majority partner, NNPC was liable for a commensurate share of gas reinjection facilities. Initially it could not meet its share of costs, and eventually, it was unable to do so on the scale previously envisaged.[4]

Recently the official position on gas flaring and utilisation has undergone a definite shift. Under the 1998 Budget the government pledged to provide incentives to businesses wishing to invest in the economic utilisation of the gas being flared. Incentives include duty and VAT free importation of

---

[2] Now Chevron

[3] See Y. Omorogbe, "An Appraisal of Nigerian Natural Gas Legislation," Vol. 4 Issue 2 *Oil and Gas Law and Taxation Review*, 51.

[4] See *Nigerian Petroleum News*, June 1995 at p 4.

machinery and equipment, tax holiday for seven years, zero percent royalty, zero percent petroleum profits tax for gas used, tax deductions on loans for gas projects, investment capital allowances, and tax free dividends for a period of five years. The gas flaring penalty was increased to ₦10 per 1,000 cubic ft. with effect from 1st January, 1998. The present government, which has been in place since May 29, 1999 has announced its intention to increase the penalty to ₦20. Operators are resistant to this as they claim that they will be paying $100 million a year as a flaring penalty. It should be noted that only the companies pay the penalty, and not the NNPC, even though both are joint venture partners[5] who are obligated to share expenses and profits in accordance with their participation interests.

The fiscal regime

The fiscal regime for natural gas differs markedly from that pertaining to crude oil, and is discussed in Topic VI below. Generally, several incentives exist to encourage investors into this area and therefore one finds that the fiscal terms are very generous.

Natural gas projects in Nigeria

Nigeria has now realised the importance of a viable natural gas industry, because of the potential foreign exchange earnings, and has actively initiated major natural gas projects. One of these is the Oso Condensate Project: the first phase of

[5] See Alexander's Gas & Oil Connections, http://www.gasandoil.com

which was commissioned in 1992. Another is the Nigerian LNG Project, which commenced its first shipments of liquefied natural gas in October, 1999. Another major project is the West Africa gas pipeline project which is transnational in scope. Yet another project is the Escravos Gas Project.

The Oso condensate project

This project, in its totality, comprises the development of the Oso condensate field and the recovery of natural gas liquids.

The Oso condensate field is in an oil mining lease in Akwa Ibom State, operated by Mobil. The development of this field was as a result of the need to utilise natural gas. Natural gas is re-injected into the reservoir in order to maximise the condensate recovery. Condensate produced is sold to further boost Nigerian oil revenues. (Condensate is not regarded as falling within the OPEC quota.) This project came on stream in 1992.

The natural gas liquids recovery project is the second phase of the project and is aimed at processing gas produced from the Oso condensate field, so as to obtain NGL. The project is estimated to produce 50,000 barrels per day of mixed propane/butane that will be exported as liquefied petroleum gas (LPG). The project involves the construction of an offshore platform, a 42km pipeline to transport the gas to Bonny, and a fractionation plant in Bonny to process the NGL into propane, butane and pentane.

The Escravos gas project

This project is the first major project to gather and utilise Nigeria's offshore gas for both local and export use. It is operated by Chevron Nigeria Limited on behalf of the NNPC/Chevron joint venture and is located at Escravos, Delta State, Nigeria.

Under this project associated gas from the Okan and Meta[6] fields in OML 90 is utilised. The gas is compressed and piped to a liquid extraction plant which removes liquefied petroleum gas (LPG) and condensate. The LPG is exported by pipeline to an offshore floating storage and Offloading vessel (FSO). The Condensate is blended with the Escravos crude oil stream, while the remaining dry gas is sold to the Nigerian Gas Company (NGC). Dry gas is better for industrial use than raw unprocessed gas, which is wet and tends to cause operation and maintenance problems.

The liquefied natural gas (LNG) project

The LNG Project is the most publicised natural gas project in Nigeria, possibly because of its total cost of $3.8 billion. Another reason must be that it has been at some stage of planning or implementation since 1976. Nigerian Liquefied Natural Gas Limited (NLNG) has commenced operations with export of LNG from the completed liquefaction plant in Bonny, Rivers State. The first shipment took place in October, 1999.[7]

---

[6] These fields are about 12km from Escravos, with combined gas reserves estimated at 5.3 trillion cubic feet. Source: *The Escravos Gas Project* published by the Public Affairs Department, Chevron Nigeria Limited. Phase I was completed in 1997 at a cost of $550 million. Phase II is more than half completed. The total project is estimated at $1 billion.

[7] There was a delay as a result of community disturbances which resulted in the LNG Plant being shut. See Topic X below).

The company is exporting to the following European buyers; ENEL (Italy), ENAGAS (Spain), Botas (Turkey), Gaz de France (France) and Transgas (Portugal). NLNG Limited is jointly owned by NNPC, Shell, Agip and Elf.

The LNG decrees

The LNG project has two enactments, which are intended to insulate it from the prevailing investment and political climate in Nigeria, and from control by various bodies, conflicting rules and bureaucratic delays. These laws are:

- Nigeria LNG (Fiscal Incentives, Guarantees and Assurances) Decree No. 39 of 1990, and
- Nigeria LNG (Fiscal Incentives Guarantees and Assurances) (Amendment) Decree No. 113 of 1993.

Fiscal details of these laws are given in topic VII below. The reader might also like to read an article on this topic in the bibliography.[8] In the light of the above examples, one should consider how efficacious it is to attempt to 'legislate' stability into existence.

The West African gas pipeline project

This $800 million project is a joint venture between Nigeria, Benin, Togo, Ghana and Chevron. It involves the utilisation of associated gas that would otherwise be flared. It is a very significant project for two main reasons. First, it is a major example of inter-African regional co-operation. Second, since

---

[8] Y. Omorogbe, "Law and Investor Protection in the Nigerian Natural Gas Industry", Vol. 14 No 2 *JERL* 179.

it is using significant amounts of associated gas it will be instrumental to the global reduction of emissions which are deleterious to the environment. Therefore it could very well be regarded as a Clean Development Mechanism (CDM) project under the terms of the Climate Change Convention. (See Topic X below)

Selected reading materials

Y. Omorogbe, "The Question of the Ownership of Natural Gas in Nigeria," (1988/89) 3 *Oil and Gas Law and Taxation Review* 75.

Y. Omorogbe, "Law and Investor Protection in the Nigerian Natural Gas Industry", Vol. 14, No.2. *Journal of Energy and National Resources Law* (JERL), 179.

Y. Omorogbe, "Investment Guarantees and Incentives in the Natural Gas Industry," Vol. 2, No.3, *Modern Practice Journal of Finance and Investment Law*, p. 142

Topic VI

Fiscal matters pertaining to the petroleum industry

Fiscal matters relating to crude oil

The oil industry is a major revenue earner for the state, mainly through the following sources:

- participating interest percentages from the joint venture
- production sharing percentages from the production sharing contract
- taxes
- royalties
- bonuses
- rents, bank charges/commissions and other payments.

Participating interest percentage

The Nigerian government, through the Nigerian National Petroleum Corporation, is a majority shareholder in all the joint ventures (JV) in Nigeria, which are dealt with under

Topic IV. Accordingly, the government receives the revenues accruing from its percentage of oil produced under these legal arrangements. This participating interest percentage is a major source of revenue for Nigeria, and is quite separate from the amounts it receives from taxation, royalties, etc. These latter amounts accrue to the government in its capacity as owner/regulator, whilst the participating interest percentage is the governments share as a business partner in the joint venture.

Production sharing percentage

Under production sharing contracts the production is split between the parties, after costs, taxes and other expenses have been paid. Each PSC partner is entitled to its own share of production and to the proceeds of sale. The government percentage is a source of revenue for the state. It is not presently very significant as most of the PSCs have not commenced production. See Topic IV for greater detail.

Taxes

Taxes are a major means of earning revenue. Petroleum tax is usually quite high because of the high economic rents that tend to accrue during periods of high prices. In Nigeria, oil taxation is governed by the Petroleum Profits Tax Act 1959, Cap 354, Laws of the Federation of Nigeria 1990 (PPTA), and the Deep Offshore and Inland Basin Production Sharing Contract Decree 1999. The latter law governs Nigerian production sharing contracts. Natural gas taxation is governed by the laws regulating liquefied natural gas (LNG) and the Associated Gas Framework Agreement (AGFA).

The PPTA applies only to the taxation of incomes of companies engaged in petroleum operations. 'Petroleum operations' is defined in S. 2 of the PPTA as follows:

> the winning or obtaining and transportation of petroleum or chargeable oil in Nigeria by or on behalf of a company for its account by any drilling, extracting or other like operations or process, not including refining at a refinery in the course of a business carried on by the company engaged in such operations, and all operations incidental thereto and any sale of or any disposal of chargeable oil by or on behalf of the company.

Taxes are levied on the profits of an accounting period. According to S.2 an accounting period runs from 1 January to 31 December, except for companies just commencing, or winding up business. The accounting period for the first year for those who are just starting runs from the date of commencement to December 31st following. For those who are ceasing business, the final accounting period will be from 1st January to the date on which they actually cease business.

The profits of the accounting period comprise a total of the proceeds of sale of all oil and natural gas (see S.9). This is not however the amount that the tax percentage will be applied to, because this amount includes monies spent and investments made by the company and cannot yet be called 'profits'. Certain deductions must therefore be made before the tax rate can be ascertained.

Adjusted profits

First the amounts which have been 'wholly, exclusively, and necessarily incurred, whether within or without Nigeria' must be deducted (see S.10). These include:

(a) land and building rent
(b) damage claims and compensation paid
(c) royalty for exported chargeable oil
(d) interest on money borrowed and used for petroleum operations.
(e) costs for repair, renewal and alteration of premises, plants, machinery etc, used for petroleum operations. Note that only money spent on repairs may be deducted. Capital for improvements may *not* be deducted here.
(f) bad debts owed to the company.
(g) 'intangible drilling costs', i.e. incidental costs associated with drilling, such as labour, fuel repairs, maintenance, hauling, etc. (see S.2 PPTA).
(h) contributions to provident funds, pension and death benefit plans for company employees.
(i) Imposts, stamp duties, fees and rates payment to local, state and federal authorities. This does *not* apply to customs duties.

At this stage, the following deductions are specifically disallowed:

(a) any disbursement, expenses or liabilities of any sort not 'wholly and exclusively' incurred for the purpose of the. petroleum operations;
(b) capital expenses, including capital utilised for improvement;
(c) sums recoverable under insurance or contracts of indemnity;

(d) Taxes of any sort, whether local or foreign;
(e) depreciation of premises, buildings, structures, works of a permanent nature, plant, machinery or fixtures;
(f) payments to any funds not approved by the Board of Inland Revenues;
(g) royalties or other sums which are deductible at a later stage, under the provisions of S.17;
(h) Expenditure to information 'relating to the existence and extent of petroleum deposits.'

The amount left after all the deductions have been made, is referred to as the *adjusted profits*.

Assessable profits

Assessable profits are adjusted profits from which any business losses have been deducted. The losses may have been made during an earlier accounting period. Where there has been a purchase and transfer from foreign to Nigerian ownership, any losses incurred by the new owner may be deducted at this stage.

Chargeable profits

To get chargeable profits, capital expenses under the provisions of the second schedule are deducted from the assessable profits. There is a limit to the amount deductible under this head. However, any outstanding amounts may be deducted during future accounting periods. Chargeable profits are the profits upon which tax may validly be levied.

Assessable tax

At this stage the tax rate is applied to the total chargeable profits of the accounting period. The normal petroleum profits tax rate as specified under the Act is 85%. For new fields, the rate is 65.75% before production, and 85% after production has commenced. For production sharing contracts in respect of shallow water concessions the tax rate is 65.75% for the first five years before production. After production the rate of 85% applies. For deepwater production sharing contractors and those with areas in the Anambra, Benin, Benue, Chad, Gongola, Sokoto and any other basins as may be determined by the Minister of Petroleum Resources, a flat rate of 50% applies. The appropriate percentage of the chargeable profits is known as the assessable tax. There are still some possible deductions after this stage. If these deductions do not apply to a company, then the figure for assessable tax will be same as the amount of chargeable tax, i.e. the amount actually paid as tax to the government.

Chargeable tax

Chargeable tax is the amount that is actually paid as tax by the company to the Government. It is arrived at after the deductions allowable under S.17 of the PPTA are.

Deductions allowed include:

(a) royalties for locally disposed chargeable oil.
(b) all non-productive rents (see S.2)

(c) specified customs and excise duties in respect of plant, storage tanks, pipelines, tools, machinery and equipment essential for use in the companies operations.

(d) investment tax credits as permitted under Paragraph 5, 2nd Schedule, PPTA.

The final amount arrived at is known as the *chargeable tax* and is paid to the government.

Tax computation simplified

Profits of the Accounting Period

Necessary recurrent expenses incurred which are necessary and/or incidental to companies petroleum operations.

= Adjusted Profits minus Losses incurred by the company.

= Assessable Profits minus Capital expenses

= CHARGEABLE PROFITS i.e. profits to which the applicable tax rate can now be applied.

85% or 65.75% or 50%, as the case may be of chargeable profits.

= Assessable Tax minus S.17 deductions

= CHARGEABLE TAX i.e. the money that is actually paid to the government as tax.

Royalties

Royalties are amounts payable to the owner of a natural resource as compensation for the exploitation of a renewable and irreplaceable natural resource. Royalty payments in

Nigeria have been amended by the Petroleum (Drilling and Production) Amendment Regulations 1995. Offshore royalties rates are also to be found in the Deep Offshore and Inland Basin Production Sharing Contract Decree No. 9 of 1999.

Onshore		20%
Offshore	0 - 100 metres	18.5%
	100 - 200 metres	16.67%
	201 - 500 metres	12.00%
	501 - 800 metres	8.00%
	801 - 1000 metres	4.00%
	> 1000 metres	0%

These graded royalties reflect the increased difficulties and higher technology and expertise necessary for deepwater production.

Bonuses

A bonus is a payment made by a company to the state at agreed designated periods. Invariably bonus payments are made when the contract has been signed. Such a bonus is known as a signature bonus. Another common payment is the production bonus, which is paid by the contractor to the state when production reaches mutually agreed levels.

Signature bonuses are sometimes regarded as onerous by the companies because they are additional pre-discovery costs that increase initial expenditure. However, the company perception of both signature and production bonuses depends on the type of discovery made or anticipated and the prevailing economic climate. Thus, Angolan offshore blocks awarded in 1998 and 1999 attracted signature bonuses as high as $200 million. This is because the companies are anticipating the discovery of large billion – barrel deposits. In such instances, these payments are not regarded as significant. However when the discovery is small and uneconomic, then such payments could render the whole profit unprofitable.

Production sharing contracts in Nigeria are subject to non-refundable signature bonus payments. For the 1991 bidding round the prospective contractor companies paid bonuses of $1 million each. For the 1999 production sharing contracts which were cancelled by the Obasanjo government, the signature bonus was $20 million.

Rents

These are amounts paid in exchange for the oil prospecting licenses and oil mining leases granted. They are as specified in para. 31, Sch. 1, 1969, and Reg. 59(2) Petroleum (Drilling and Production) Regulations 1969.

Rents paid for non-producing areas are credited 100% against petroleum profits tax. Rents for producing leases are credited 85% against royalty payments.

Other payments such as bank commissions are paid by the oil companies. The government also derives money from the industry indirectly through enactments such as the Oil Terminal Dues Act. Note however that payments made under this law are by the master or owner of the ship evacuating crude oil and not by the oil producing company.

Fiscal matters relating to natural gas

The LNG decrees

The Nigeria LNG (Fiscal Incentives Guarantees and Assurances) Decree No. 39 of 1990 , and Nigeria LNG (Fiscal Incentives, Guarantees and Assurances) (Amendment) Decree No. 113 of 1993 are exclusively for the benefit of the liquefied natural gas project.

Section 1 of the principal decree confers pioneer status on Nigeria LNG Limited, in accordance with the provisions of the Industrial Development (Income Tax Relief) Act 1971. Section 2 provides for a 10-year tax relief period and section 3 provides that the company shall be subject to the Companies Income Tax Act 1979, and not the Petroleum Profits Tax Act 1959. All accounting is to be done in United States dollars. Interest on loans is to be fully deductible for tax purposes. Tax is not payable on the categories of money specified in section 6, which include interest paid on loans made by foreign companies, and earnings of non-Nigerian companies or citizens. By the amending decree, the provisions of the National Shipping Policy Decree 1987, are declared inapplicable to the company and its contractors, subcontractors, customers, or any shipping concern involved with the company's trade in LNG. The company is totally exempted from all customs duties, levies, charges and imposts of a similar nature. In addition, the provisions of the Pre-Shipment Inspection of Imports Act are specifically stated not to apply "in relation to the importation of a plant, machinery, goods and materials for use in the construction of or incorporation of a plant, jetty, shipping, transmission facilities and ancillary works used in the Company's business and in respect of any major spare parts needed in the event of a plant failure and ordered within two years of the commissioning of that plant for which the spare part is ordered." In addition, "no export duties, taxes or other duties, levies, charges or impost of a similar nature shall be payable or imposed on the export of liquefied natural gas or other hydrocarbons produced by the company."

Of particular significance is the second schedule which is entitled "Guarantees and Assurances to Nigeria LNG Limited and its Shareholders." The preamble to this schedule provides that;

> The Federal Government of the Federal Republic of Nigeria ('the Government') in recognition of the magnitude of, and in consideration of the investments which shall have to be made in order to prosecute the Venture described in the shareholders' contract dated 19th May 1989 between the Nigerian National Petroleum Corporation , Shell gas BV, CLEAG Limited, and Agip International BV, as amended from time to time (such shareholders' contract, as so amended in this Decree referred to as the Contract) hereby grants to the Company, its successors and to each of the shareholders from time to time (in their capacity as such), the Guarantees, Assurances and Undertakings following hereunder. These Guarantees, Assurances and Undertakings shall have effect from the date hereof and so long as the Company or any successor hereto, is in existence and carrying on the business of liquefying and selling liquefied natural gas and natural gas liquids within and/or outside the Federal Republic of Nigeria.

The government binds itself to do nothing to render invalid or unenforceable rights and obligations arising under the contract and "other contracts and arrangements contemplated in the contract." It further binds itself not to amend the fiscal regime contained within this Decree, except with the prior written agreement of the shareholders, Nigeria LNG and itself. In addition, the company and its shareholders shall not be subject to new laws, regulations, taxes, etc., which are not generally applicable to companies incorporated in Nigeria. Again, the government "agrees to ensure that these Guarantees shall not be suspended, modified or revoked during the life of the Venture, except with the mutual consent of the Government and shareholders."

The rest of the Schedule consists mostly of ways and means by which the government shall help the company by aiding it with facilities, such as phone and telex services, and the dredging and maintenance of the Bonny bar channel. Para 15 provides that "for all practical purposes the Company shall be treated as an independent, autonomous, commercial entity and its operations, policies, procedures and conditions of services shall be determined by the Board of Directors of the Company." Para 21 recognises the shareholders' "right to prompt, adequate and effective compensation in the event of expropriation of tangible property or property rights or interference with contract rights." The final paragraph is on modalities 'for dispute settlement with respect to the provisions of this Decree. Where the dispute cannot be amicably settled within 90 days, "such dispute may be submitted to arbitration before the International Centre for the Settlement of Investment Disputes."

The associated gas framework agreement and other gas incentives

Most incentives relating to gas are under the Associated Gas Framework Agreement (AGFA), or are contained in past budget pronouncements.

AGFA came into existence in 1992, to encourage investment in the natural gas sector. Under this agreement PPT for gas was set at 40%. The 1998 budget speech reduced this to the Company income tax rate of 30%. Capital allowances are 20% for the first four years, and 19% in the fifth year with a 1% retention. A three year tax holiday was granted under AGFA. This was increased to 5 years in the 1998 budget. Royalty on gas is 7% onshore and 5% offshore. Where gas is being transferred either from an upstream to a downstream location or from a natural gas liquid extraction facility to a gas-to-liquid facility, no royalty is payable. The latter incentive was granted under the 1999 budget.

The practice of amending a law by extra legal means is certainly not to be condoned. It is, however, unlikely to occur under a democratic regime as it is a practice unrecognised by law.

The memorandum of understanding

The Memorandum of Understanding (MOU) came about as a result of the slump in the oil market in the 1980s. The companies profit margins were eroded as a result of which they slowed down on their exploration and production activities in Nigeria.

The MOU is a legal arrangement between the federal government and each of the producing companies, aimed at encouraging these companies to continually explore and produce in Nigeria. In return for this the government guarantees these companies a stipulated profit margin irrespective of market conditions.

The first MOU was signed in 1986 and the second one in 1991. The former guaranteed a profit margin of $2.00 per barrel while the latter guaranteed $2.30 per barrel, after tax and royalty payments. This was achieved by modifying the fiscal regime through the utilisation of a pricing formula. The existing MOU was signed in July 2000. This agreement, which is the third, provides for a two-tier profit margin of $2.50 and $2.70. The higher margin is for companies whose unit investments are more than $2/bbl. For those with lower investment amounts the lower figure is applicable. Other features include:

- an increase in the oil companies' technical costs from $3.50 to $4.00 per barrel and the decoupling of fiscal operating costs of $2/bbl.
- a 35% tax rate to reduce excessive operating costs
- the capex element of ullage fees are to be excluded from the penalised actual operating cost and aligned with the actual capital technical costs.

The effects of the MOU have generally been positive, particularly when one realises that without it, profits for the oil companies would have dropped as low as $1.00 or even 80 cents a barrel. These low amounts would be great disincentives to the viability of the industry and to continued exploration efforts in the country.

Selected reading materials

G. Etikerentse: "Responsibilities and Profits in Oil and Gas Industry" presented at Workshop on Essentials of Oil and Gas Law" organised by the Centre for Petroleum Environment and Development Studies (CEPEDS), Lagos 22 – 24 September, 1998.[1]

Kemi Segun, "Fiscal Incentives, Tax Investment, presented at the Symposium on "Oil and Gas Investments in Nigeria" organised by CWC Associates, London 14th May, 1999.[2]

M. M. Olisa, *Nigerian Petroleum, Law and Practice*, Chap. 5.

[1] Obtainable at CEPEDS, 27 McNeil Road, Yaba.

[2] Obtainable at Adepetun, Caxton Martins and Agbor, 27 Strachan Street, Lagos

Topic VII

The Organization of the Petroleum Exporting Countries (OPEC)

History, aims and objectives

The Organisation of Petroleum Exporting Countries (OPEC) was established in September 1960 by the five founding countries, Iran, Iraq, Saudi Arabia, Kuwait and Venezuela. This organisation has fundamentally influenced the growth and direction of the international oil industry.

OPEC has been described as being born of protest against the behaviour of the multinational oil companies. These companies totally dominated the oil industry, at the expense of the oil producing host countries. They dictated how much oil was extracted, how much was sold, who the oil was sold to, and the price at which it was sold. Not only did the host countries have no say in the industry, they received very little in return for the oil produced. No taxes were paid initially. The royalty paid was little, was based on weight and volume rather than on price, and was expensed by the companies when tax rates started to be applied.

The final crunch came in 1959, when the companies unilaterally cut the posted prices for Venezuelan crude by \$0.05/b and for Middle Eastern by \$0.18/b. In August 1960 further reductions ranging between \$0.1 and \$0.14 per barrel were made. Whilst these amounts appear quite small, they amounted to sizeable reductions in revenue for the oil producing states. In reaction to these price cuts a meeting of oil producing states was convened in the following month, in Baghdad, Iraq. It was attended by representatives of the governments of Iran, Iraq, Kuwait, Saudi Arabia and Venezuela. At this meeting, the Organisation of Petroleum Exporting Countries (OPEC) was formed.

Article 2 of the OPEC Statute lists the principal aims and objectives of the organisation:

> Article 2
>
> The principal aim of the Organisation shall be the co-ordination and unification of the petroleum policies of Member Countries and the determination of the best means for safeguarding their interests, individually and collectively.
>
> The Organisation shall devise ways and means of ensuring the stabilisation of prices in international oil markets with a view to eliminating harmful and unnecessary fluctuations.
>
> Due regard shall be given at all times to the interests of the producing nations and to the necessity of securing a steady income to the producing countries; an efficient, economic and regular supply of petroleum to consuming

nations; and a fair return on their capital to those investing in the petroleum industry.

From this article, OPEC's stated aims and objectives centre around price stabilisation. However, OPEC has been concerned with the growth of the petroleum industries' also of its member countries, and with development issues. At the OPEC conference of Sovereigns and Heads of State in 1966, Member Countries adopted the 'Solemn Declaration'.
This Declaration stated that OPEC should seek, in co-operation with other countries, for the creation of a New International Economic Order based on justice, mutual understanding and genuine concern for the well-being of all peoples of the world.

It called on industrialised and developing countries to co-operate to solve the problems of poor nations and to establish a more equitable economic order. Amongst other things, the Declaration determined that the interests of OPEC member countries required that oil prices should take into account the following:

- the imperatives of conservation of petroleum, including its depletion and increasing scarcity in the future.
- the value of oil in terms of its non-energy use, and
- the conditions of availability, utilisation and costs of alternative sources of energy.

Membership

The OPEC Statute[1] provides that any country which is a substantial net exporter of crude oil and which has

---

[1] Article 7c.

'fundamentally similar interests' to those of member countries, may become a full member if it is accepted by three quarters of the full members of the organisation, including the founding members. The statute does not define the qualities that a country needs to be considered as a net exporter so one can conclude that this matter is entirely at the discretion of the Conference.

As to having fundamentally similar interests, opinions have been expressed as to what these might be.
One of OPEC's founding fathers, Perez Alfonso[2] of Venezuela, has stated that one common interest amongst members was the necessity of protecting themselves from the 'powerful' international industry which was then in control of the resource. Dr. Rouhani, the first OPEC Secretary–General has deduced what the common interest might be by reviewing the common interests of the five founding members, and conditions common to them when OPEC was created. According to him, these are the following:[3]

(1) the founder members were developing countries.
(2) they were large exporters of oil.
(3) they were dependent on their oil revenues for the financing of their budgets.
(4) they needed the assistance of foreigners for the exploitation of their oil resources and therefore, their oil industry was in the hands of the major oil companies.
(5) the agreements governing the operation of their oil industries were similar. For this reason, the problems and

---

[2] M.S. Al-Otaiba, *OPEC and the Petroleum Industry*, Croom Helm, 1972, chap. 8 at p.79

[3] *Op. cit.* at pp. 79 - 80

disputes that arose between the host countries and the operating companies were often identical.

Dr. Mana Saeed Al-Olaiba identifies another common interest' which is:

> the common feeling of bitterness inherited by the people of these countries and which had grown in consequence of the injustices inflicted by the inequitable oil concessions granted to the companies. There was therefore a common interest in easing the consequences of injustice and remedying the situation.[4]

As mentioned earlier, OPEC was created by the first five founding members - Iran, Iraq, Kuwait, Saudi Arabia - at the Baghdad Conference of 10-14, September 1960. Over the years eight other countries joined the organisation: Qatar (1961); Indonesia (1962); Libya (1962); United Arab Emirates (1967); Algeria (1969); Nigeria (1971); Ecuador (1973); and Gabon (1975).

Ecuador, at its own requests, had its membership 'suspended' from 31 December, 1992. Interestingly the OPEC statute only refers to withdrawal and not suspension in Article 8 where it states:

> No Member of the Organisation may withdraw from membership without giving notice of its intention to do so to the Conference. Such notice shall take effect at the beginning of the next calendar year after the date of its receipt by the Conference, subject to the Member having at that time fulfilled all financial obligations arising out of its membership.

---

[4] *Op. cit.*

> In the event of any country having ceased to be a Member of the Organisation, its readmission to membership shall be made in accordance with Article 7, paragraph C.

From official statements of OPEC,[5] "the OPEC Conference regretfully accepted the wish of Ecuador to suspend its Full Membership of the Organisation. However, the Conference hoped that Ecuador would be able to overcome the economic constraints facing it and rejoin the Organisation in the not–too-distant future."

OPEC is composed of Arab and non-Arab states, and of Muslim and secular states. Members are from four separate geographic regions. Therefore, can one still speak of fundamentally similar interests? The opinion here is that it can still be said that fundamental interests, that is, interests common to all members, exist. The belief is that these interests are responsible for the continued existence of the organisation. OPEC has withstood serious internal conflicts such as war between two members (Kuwait and Iraq). It has also withstood several attempts from outside to undermine its work and efforts. In fact, a whole organisation, the International Energy Agency, came into existence to counteract the hold that OPEC once exercised over the international oil industry.

The fundamental interests which continue to sustain OPEC centre around the realisation of the importance of OPEC to its members and the important and positive role that it has played and continues to play in the positive evolution of their respective oil industries. The fact is that an organisation which controls more than three – quarters

---

5 "A Brief History of OPEC", P.6 at the OPEC Website http://www.opec.org.

of the worlds reserves and which has nine out of ten of the world's biggest oil producers, cannot be overlooked.[6] The members realise this, and the organisation continues.

Organs of OPEC

OPEC has three main organs: the Conference, the Board of Governors and the Secretariat.

The Conference

The Conference is the 'supreme authority' of the organisation. It consists of the Heads of Delegations of member countries, usually the Ministers of Petroleum. It meets twice a year, and decisions, other than on procedural matters, require the unanimous agreement of all members. However the absence of a full member at a meeting does not prevent a Resolution from becoming effective unless the Secretariat receives a notification to the contrary from the said Member, at least ten days before the date fixed for publication of the Resolutions.

The Conference has the following functions:[7]

- to formulate the general policy of the organisation and determine the appropriate ways and means of its implementation;
- to decide upon any application for membership of the organisation;
- to confirm the appointment of members of the board of governors;
- to direct the board of governors to submit reports or make recommendations on any matters of interest to the organisation;

---

[6] See pp. 94 – 95 below

[7] Article 15.

- to consider, or decide upon, the reports and recommendations submitted by the board of governors on the affairs of the organisation;
- to consider and decide upon the budget of the organisation, as submitted by the board of governors;
- to consider and decide upon the statement of accounts and the auditor's report, as submitted by the board of governors;
- to call a Consultative Meeting for such member countries, for such purposes, and in such places, as the Conference deems fit;
- to approve any amendments to this Statute;
- to appoint the chairman of the board of governors and an alternate chairman;
- to appoint the secretary-general;
- to appoint the deputy secretary-general; and
- to appoint the auditor of the organisation for a duration of one year.

The board of governors

The board of governors is composed of governors nominated by member countries for terms of two years. The board meets twice a year. It is the organ that effectively manages OPEC.

The board of governors shall;[8]

- direct the management of the affairs of the organisation and the implementation of the decisions of the Conference;
- consider and decide upon any reports submitted by the secretary-general;
- submit reports and make recommendations to the Conference on the affairs of the organisation;

---

[8] Article 20

- draw up the budget of the organisation for each calendar year and submit it to the Conference for approval;
- nominate the auditor of the organisation for a duration of one year;
- consider the Statement of Accounts and the Auditor's Report and submit them to the Conference for approval;
- approve the appointment of directors of divisions and heads of departments, upon nomination by the member countries, due consideration being given to the recommendations of the secretary-general;
- convene an Extraordinary Meeting of the Conference;
- prepare the agenda for the Conference.

The Secretariat and the Secretary-General[9]

The secretariat is to carry out the executive functions of the organisation in accordance with the provisions of this statute and under the direction of the board of governors. The Secretary General is the legally authorised representative of OPEC and the chief officer of the Secretariat. He is appointed on merit for a term of three years renewable once for the same period, by the unanimous decision of the Conference. If there is a failure to obtain a unanimous decision, then the Secretary General shall be appointed on a rotational basis for a two - year term. He must be a national of one of the member countries and must meet the following minimum conditions:[10]

- 35 years of age.
- A degree from a recognised university in law, economics, science, engineering or business administration.

---

[9] Articles. 25 - 35
[10] Article 28

- 15 years experience, of which at least 10 years should have been spent in positions directly related to the oil industry, and five years in highly responsible executive or managerial positions. Experience in government-company relations and in the international aspects of the oil industry is desirable.

The first secretary-general was appointed in 1961. Since then there have been seventeen secretaries-general, up until October 1999. Two of these have been Nigerians, Chief Feyide and Dr. Lukman. The full list is as follows:

1.	Dr. Fuad Rouhani 21/1/61 - 30/4/64	Iran
2.	Abdul Rahman Al-Bazzazi 1/5/64 - 30/4/65	Iraq
3.	Ashraf Lutf 1/5/65 - 31/12/66	Kuwait
4.	Mohammad Saleh Joukhdar 1/1/67 - 31/12/67	Saudi Arabia
5.	Francisco R. Parra 1/1/68 - 31/12/68	Venezuela
6.	Dr. Elrich Sanger 1/1/69 - 31/12/69	Indonesia
7.	Omar El Badri 1/1/70 - 31/12/70	SP Libyan AJ
8.	Dr. Nadim Pachachi 1/1/71 - 31/12/72	UAE
9.	Dr. Abderrahman Khene 1/1/73 - 31/12/74	Algeria
10.	Chief M.O. Feyide 1/1/75 - 31/12/76	Nigeria
11.	Ali M. Jaidah 1/1/77 - 31/12/78	Qatar

12.	Rene G. Ortiz 1/1/79 - 30/6/81	Ecuador
13.	Dr. Marc Saturnin Nan Nguema 1/7/81 - 30/6/83	Gabon
14.	Dr. Fadhil J. Al-Chalabi 1/7/83 - 30/6/88	Iraq
15.	Dr. Subroto 1/7/88 - 30/6/94	Indonesia
16.	Abdalla Salem El Badri 1/7/94 - 31/12/94	SP Libyan AJ
17.	Dr. Rilwanu Lukman 1/1/95 - date	Nigeria

Departments of OPEC

The OPEC Statute provides for the creation of:

- a Division of Research
- the Personnel and Administration Department
- the Public Information Department.

The Division of Research is responsible for continuous research in line with the needs of the organisation 'placing particular emphasis on energy and related matters.' It consists of three departments; the Energy Studies Department, the Economics and Finance Department and the Data Services Department.

The Personnel and Administration Department is responsible for all organisational methods, the provision of administrative services for all meetings, personnel matters, budgets, accounting and internal· control. It studies and reviews general administrative policies and industrial relations methods used in the industry, in member and other countries and advises members as to possible improvements. It is also to keep abreast of current administrative policies and for policy changes occurring in the international petroleum industry which might affect or interest OPEC.

The Public Information Department is responsible for presenting "OPEC objectives, decisions and actions in their true and most desirable perspective" in carrying out a central public information programme and identifying suitable areas for the promotion of OPEC's aims; and producing and distributing publications and other matters. This Department publishes the *OPEC Bulletin*, which is essential reading for anyone wishing to acquire up-to-date knowledge of the international oil industry.

Other departments in OPEC are:

- The Office of the Secretary-General, which gives executive assistance to the Secretary-General.
- The Legal Office which provides legal advice and services to the secretary-general, supervises the Secretariat's legal and contractual affairs, evaluates legal issues of concern to OPEC and its member countries, and makes recommendations for appropriate action.
- The OPEC News Agency (OPECNA). This disseminates news in OPEC and other Third World countries, and features or reports matters of interest to them. It is increasingly used by specialised publications and the general media.

The OPEC Fund for International Development (OFID)

The OPEC Fund for International Development (OFID) was established in 1976 by the member countries of OPEC. Its fundamental objective is to promote South/South solidarity through financial co-operation between OPEC members and other developing countries. The Fund's headquarters are also located in Vienna. It is however a separate institution from OPEC, with its own management and organisational structure.

The resources of the Fund consist of voluntary contributions by the member countries, and accumulated income derived from the Funds Investments and loans. Aid from Fund is unique in that it is "aid without strings". In other words, unlike aid from practically every other aid institution in the world, it is not tied to procurement from the donors.

All developing countries, with the exception of OPEC member countries, are eligible for loans from the Fund. However priority is given to the least developed countries. Over the years the Funds has given loans to 105 countries, of which 48 are in Africa, 31 in Asia, 23 in Latin America and the Caribbean, and 3 in Europe.

The Fund has so far implemented twelve lending programmes. The thirteenth lending programme is for a 2 year period from January 1, 1998 to December 1999. By the end of December 1998 US $3,982.7 million had been committed in the form of 778 loans. Also 478 grants, totalling US $240.9 million had been made. This latter amount includes the contributions of 35 least – developed countries to the Common Fund for Commodities (CFC); a voluntary contribution to the Second Account of the CFC; and a special contribution of US $20 million to the International Fund for Agricultural Development (IFAD). In totality, the Funds approved commitments as at the end of December 1998, were US $5,195.5 million.

OPEC and its contribution to the development of oil and gas law

OPEC has played an important role in the development of the international oil industry through the promotion of policies and actions aimed at strengthening and empowering developing countries so that they would be able to exercise meaningful control over their oil resources.

One of OPEC's most important resolutions was resolution XVI. 90 adopted on June 24 1968 and published on July 24, 1968. It was titled 'Declaratory Statement of Petroleum Policy in Member Countries. This resolution stated ten principles, all aimed at improving the legal and regulatory framework for the oil industries' of the member countries.

OPEC also played a key role in the establishment of national oil companies in its member countries. This was seen as essential if meaningful control was to be achieved. The establishment of the Nigerian National Oil Corporation was a direct response to OPEC calls for member countries to establish national oil companies (NOCs) which would be vehicles for state participation in the oil industry.

The new contracts for exploration and development have evolved because of the desire of host countries to shift away from investor ownership of a natural resource, towards ownership and control by the owners of the oil resources. OPEC is the main body behind this trend. Without the Organisation, one can safely say that the legal regime regulating oil and gas would be widely different.

OPEC has expressed a desire for the unification of petroleum laws in member countries. This is yet to be achieved but a perusal of history and possible future trends leads one to know that this could become a possibility in the future.

A critical evaluation of OPEC

OPEC is forty years old. It is an organisation which has fundamentally affected the world in which we live today, and the international oil industry.

At its creation this industry was controlled by the multinational oil corporations. By the early 1970's the industry was controlled by OPEC, and every pronouncement after an OPEC Conference was received with bated breath by the international news media. Now things are different. There are now several producers outside OPEC and therefore OPEC can no longer be said to be in control of oil prices.

However OPEC still remains a force in the international oil industry. While OPEC countries produce 40% of the world's crude oil, 60% of exported oil which is traded internationally comes from OPEC countries. As at the end of 1996, OPEC had proven reserves of 801,998 million barrels of crude oil, representing 76.6% of the world total[11] with 261,444 million barrels. Saudi Arabia alone has the worlds largest proven resources, more than twice the amount of the second largest country which is Iraq with 112,000 million barrels. Nine out of the world's ten largest producers are OPEC countries. Also, oil remains the most important source of energy, and future scenarios envisage that any reductions in the crude oil share of the international market, will be due to the growth in the use

[11] Source: OPEC Annual Statistical Bulletin 1996

of natural gas. OPEC countries also contain extensive deposits of natural gas.

With all this in mind, OPEC remains a relevant and important organisation that will continue to play a role in the international oil industry, in years to come.

Selected reading materials

Information about OPEC can be got from its website – http://www.opec.org and its publications, e.g.:

- *The OPEC Bulletin*
- *OPEC Annual Review*
- *OPEC Statute*

As a background, see Prerre Terzian *OPEC: The Inside Story* , Zed Press, 1981.

Topic VIII

National oil corporations and the Nigerian National Petroleum Corporation

History

National oil corporations have been a feature of the industry from the beginning of the twentieth century. The first few companies originated in Europe. This is as a result of the fact that World War I emphasised the strategic importance of the oil industry to any nation. It was clear that a major reason why the allies won that war was because they had access to crude oil while the Germans did not.

Initially, ownership took the form of share acquisitions. For example, the British government acquired majority shares in the Anglo-Persian Oil Company (now known as British Petroleum) in 1914. As another example Compagnie Francaise de Petroleos (CFP) was created with French equity and forty percent voting shares in the company. The first purely state - owned company in Europe is however Azienda Generale Italiana Petroli, more popularly known as AGIP. Presently, there are several of such companies to be found actively participating in the industry all over the world. One newer

NOC that has had a meteoric rise is the Norwegian oil company, Statoil, which is one of the companies operating in Nigeria today.

In the developing world, the Latin American countries were the first to form national oil companies. The very first was Yascimientos Petroliferos Fiscales of Argentina (YPF) in 1922. It does appear however, that tne Mexican NOC, Petroleos Mexicanos (PEMEX) could be said to have been more active during this initial stage, because of the Mexican nationalisations of 1938. Practically all other national oil corporations in developing countries were created after the establishment of OPEC in 1960. The major exception to this appears to be the National Iranian Oil Company (NIOC) which was formed in 1957 to give effect to the nationalisation of the Anglo - Iranian concession a few years earlier.

Now, it can be said that practically every country in the world has a national oil company, whether or not it is an oil importing or exporting country.

The rationale for the establishment of NOCs

National oil companies are created primarily to advance state objectives and policy. In this sense they differ fundamentally from a private company which is invariably set up primarily to make profits. Whilst increased revenue is important to every country, other state objectives are often just as, or even more important. A state company is expected to advance all or most of the state objectives. These include the following;

- ***Security of supplies***. A primary reason for the creation of an NOC is the necessity to ensure that the state has constant access to oil so that its energy supplies will not be impeded. This reason is common to both exporting and importing nations although it is more critical for the importers.

- ***To oversee and control the activities of the domestic oil industry***; Another primary reason is to oversee and control the activities of the oil industry by ensuring that the industry promotes state policies such as increased exploration, effecting state participation, promoting investments in the oil sector etc.
- ***To make profits***: A state invariably wishes to make profits from its oil industry, even as the policy aims outlined above are being advanced. However, the satisfaction of non-profited related state policies means that NOCs often make less profits than a purely private company would make. There is a limit as to how far profit objectives can be sacrificed in favour of policy, as the NOC can end up being run inefficiently and even becoming a drain on national resources.

A major problem that this group of companies have had is that they have often tended to promote state policy, to the detriment of all other objectives. In some instances, the state objectives that the NOC is concerned with might not even be related to oil industry issues, but to matters which the state has decided that it should be involved with. The Indonesian NOC, Pertamina, provides an example of an NOC that almost got bogged down as a result of investing in an airline, oil tankers, a rice estate, a steel complex and a fertiliser plant. As a result, despite the fact that it earned forty-nine percent of Indonesia's foreign revenue at that time (1974) it went into debt, to the tune of $10 billion.[1] This has been said to be nearly ten times the peak losses made by firms like Chrysler and Ford during

[1] Louis Turner, *Oil Companies in the International System*, George Allen & Unwin 1983, 3rd edn.

the 1979 – 81 period.[2] This trait is not peculiar to NOCs from developing countries. They have tended to exhibit such traits more, only because of the types of governments that they have often been prone to. The fact is that as long as a state maintains an economic interest in any industry, state policy is likely to affect decisions taken by the concern. As the companies are becoming commercialised and even-to an extent-becoming privatised uneconomic state policy concerns are likely to carry less weight. However, certain policy objectives, e.g. security of supply, will still be deciding factors in some instances.

Nigerian National Petroleum Corporation

The Nigerian National Petroleum Corporation (NNPC) was established in 1977 by an Act of the same name. It was formed as a result of a merger between the Ministry of Petróleum Resources, and the Nigerian National Oil Corporation which was established in 1971.

The Nigerian National Oil Corporation was established by Decree No. 18 of April 1971 'to engage in prospecting for, mining and marketing oil and all other activities with the petroleum oil ministry.' NNOC was an offshoot of the Ministry of Mines and Power and from the outset, it had problems centred around the fact of its dependency on the ministry. The initial efforts at state participation in Nigeria's oil industry were done through this Corporation.

Jurisdictional problems between NNOC and the Ministry of Mines and Power led to the creation of NNPC in 1977 through Decree No. 33. The new entity combined the commercial functions of NNOC with the regulatory functions

---

[2] Ibid.

of the Ministry. These latter functions were under the Petroleum Inspectorate which was established under part II of the Act as an integral part of the corporation.

The NNPC Act has remained in force in a largely unaltered form since it was first enacted. The affairs of the Corporation are to be conducted by a board of directors. The Act provides that the Board should be chaired by a "Minister in the Government of the Federation to be known and styled as the Minister of Petroleum Resources." According to sec 1(2) other members are:

(a) the Director-General, Federal Ministry of Finance and Economic Development;
(b) the Managing Director of the Corporation; and
(c) three persons to be appointed by the National Council of Ministers, being persons who by reason of their ability, experience or specialised knowledge of the oil industry or of business or professional attainments are capable of making useful contributions to the work of the Corporation.

NNPC's duties include participating in all stages and areas of the upstream and downstream energy sector; carrying out research in connection with petroleum; participating on the Federal Government's behalf in petroleum activities, and engaging in activities to 'enhance the petroleum industry' and to give 'full effect to the provisions' of the Act. It is worthwhile to set out NNPC's functions under the Decree in full:[3]

(a) exploring and prospecting for, working, winning or otherwise acquiring, possessing and disposing of petroleum;

[3] S. 5, Nigerian National Petroleum Act. Cap. 320, LFN 1990

(b) refining, treating, processing and generally engaging in the handling of petroleum for the manufacture and production of petroleum products and its derivatives;

(c) purchasing and marketing petroleum, its products and by-products;

(d) providing and operating pipelines, tanker-ships or other facilities for the carriage or conveyance of crude oil, natural gas and their products and derivatives, water and any other liquids or other commodities related to the corporation's operations;

(e) constructing, equipping and maintaining tank farms and other facilities for the handling and treatment of petroleum and its products and derivatives;

(f) carrying out research in connection with petroleum or anything derived from it and promoting activities for the purpose of turning to account the results of such research;

(g) doing anything required for the purpose of giving effect to agreements entered into by the Federal Government with a view to securing participation by the government or the corporation in activities connected with petroleum;

(h) generally engaging in activities that would enhance the petroleum industry in the overall interest of Nigeria; and

(i) undertaking such other activities as are necessary or expedient for giving full effect to the provisions of this Act.

Whilst the law remains essentially unchanged, NNPC has gone through three main reorganisations, none of which have not been translated into legislative realities.

The first re-organisation[4]

Following the Irikefe Commission of Enquiry set up to look into the alleged disappearance of US$2.8 billion from the account of NNPC, it was decided that the Corporation had become too large to function efficiently. Therefore, a Ministry was recreated, this time titled Petroleum and Energy. Also some subsidiaries were established. These subsidiaries were intended to be independent and self-accountable, and included the three refineries that then existed, at Port Harcourt, Kaduna and Warri. This reorganisation occurred during the first half of the decade of the 1980s.

The second re-organisation

This reorganisation occurred in 1988 and led to the separation of the Petroleum Inspectorate from NNPC, its merger with the Ministry of Petroleum, and its renaming as the Department of Petroleum Resources.

NNPC was also declared to be commercialised with the following subsidiaries:

- Eleme Petrochemicals Co. Ltd
- Warri Refining and Petrochemicals Co. Ltd
- Kaduna Refining and Petrochemicals Co. Ltd
- Port Harcourt Refining and Petrochemicals Co. Ltd
- Nigerian Petroleum Development Co. Ltd
- Integrated Data Services Ltd
- Pipelines and Products Marketing Co. Ltd
- Nigerian Gas Company Ltd

---

[4] On the reorganisation of NNPC see generally M. M. Olisa, *Nigerian Petroleum Law and Practice*, pp. 202 – 209.

- National Engineering and Technical Co. Ltd (NETCO)
- Nigeria LNG Limited
- Hyson Nigeria Limited.

Interestingly, around that time the president of Nigeria appointed eighteen persons as members of the board, notwithstanding the provisions of the NNPC Act. Since that time, the board has been dissolved and reconstituted at intervals, usually with someone other than the minister being designated chairman and usually with far more members than the law allows for. As at the time of writing there is no board.

During this period six divisions were created; Services, Upstream and Gas Development, Downstream, Finance and Accounts, Commercial and National Petroleum Investment Management Services (NAPIMS).

By a Federal Government Gazette, the Ministry of Petroleum Resources was given the following responsibilities:

(a) the overall supervision of the Nigerian petroleum industry including the Nigerian National Petroleum Corporation and its subsidiaries to ensure compliance with applicable statutes;

(b) issuing permits, licences, leases and giving authorisations and approvals prescribed by statutes for a whole range of petroleum activities from seismic surveys to drilling, production, construction and operation of process plants like refineries, petrochemical and liquefied natural gas plants and for the marketing of petroleum products;

(c) policy matters on the granting of petroleum rights and the marketing of crude oil, natural gas and their derivatives;

(d) monitoring and control of environmental pollution associated with oil and gas operations and the administration and enforcement of environmental protection statutes and statutory provisions affecting such operations;

(e) fixing of production allowables and prices for crude oil, natural gas, petroleum products and their derivatives;
(f) enforcement of oil and gas conservation laws and practices and monitoring petroleum activities to ensure proper conservation of oil and gas;
(g) giving such assistance to the petroleum industry as would enhance the industry in the overall interest of Nigeria; and
(h) duties relating to the following bodies:
- Nigerian National Petroleum Corporation,
- Organisation of Petroleum Exporting Countries,
- Petroleum Equalisation Fund,
- Petroleum Technology Development Fund,
- Petroleum Training Institute, Effurun and
- African Petroleum Producers Association.

Thus one sees a return to the dichotomy that existed during the era of the Nigerian National Oil Corporation. A comparison of NNPC's functions with those of the Ministry show that both these entities have been assigned the same duties in essence, with primacy being given to the Ministry. Thus this combination of conflicting and overlapping law and policy has created a less-than-ideal situation within which conflicts could occur.

The third re-organisation

NNPC underwent another major reorganisation around 1995 when it was restructured into six directorates each headed by an executive director:

(1) Exploration and Productions Directorate, consisting of six divisions.
  (a) NAPIMS,
  (b) NPDC Ltd,
  (c) Integrated Data Services Limited
  (d) Nigerian Gas Company Limited

(e) Crude Oil Sales Department
(f) Direct Exploration services.

(2) Refining and Petrochemicals Directorate consisting of
(a) Port Harcourt Refining Company Ltd
(b) Warri Refinery and Petrochemicals Company Ltd
(c) Kaduna Refinery and Petrochemicals Company Ltd
(d) Eleme Petrochemicals Company Ltd
(e) Petroleum Products Marketing Co. Ltd.

(3) Engineering and Technical Directorate consisting of
(a) Pipeline and Tank Construction Division with Pipelines responsibility transferred from PPMC,
(b) Research and Development Division,
(c) Engineering and Technical Division,
(d) National Engineering and Technical Company Limited,
(e) Materials Management Department headed by a General Manager;

(4) Commercial Investments Directorate consisting of
(a) Hyson/Calson Ltd
(b) a Division dealing with various downstream investments,
(c) a Division dealing with upstream service companies,
(d) Property Investments Department.

(5) Finance and Accounts Directorate with three main Divisions: Finance, Accounts and Investment.

(6) Corporate Services Directorate consisting of Administration, Medical and Legal Divisions, Central Purchasing, the Corporation's London Office, and the Insurance Unit.

The Public Affairs Division, Corporate Planning and Development Division, the Corporate Secretariat and Corporate Audit Department are under the office of the Group Managing Director.

This reorganisation can possibly be described as practical in the sense that entities and departments with similar functions are grouped together within the same directorate. However, it is doubtful whether any lawyer could have been involved in this reorganisation because a curious situation that lacks uniformity now exists. Limited liability companies co-exist side by side with internal departments, headed by managing directors and general managers respectively, and are grouped together as divisions. This situation is particularly marked in the Exploration and Production Directorate and is a legal anomaly.

The normal legal situation is to either (a) have a holding company with subsidiaries that are limited liability companies, or (b) to have an entity - parastatal or limited liability or otherwise - with internal departments or divisions.

As with all the other reorganisations there is no legal basis for this one. Therefore there is no correlation between what actually pertains in NNPC and what is to be found in the law.

Selected reading materials

Hasan Zakariya, "State Petroleum Companies" 12 *Journal of World Trade Law* (1978) 481.

Y. Omorogbe, *The Oil and Gas Industry: Exploration and Production Contracts, op. cit.* Chapter 2, 35 – 38.

M.M. Olisa: *Nigerian Petroleum Law and Practice*

The NNPC website, nnpc.com.ng. should be a major repository of information when it becomes fully functional.

Topic IX

Downstream oil and gas law and policy

Historical perspective

The downstream sector is concerned with the post-production stages of oil and gas through the refining and processing stages, until it passes to the consumer. It is a fairly vast subject and will be briefly treated here under the subheadings of transportation, refining, marketing and petrochemicals.

In this area the major applicable laws and regulations are as follows:

- Oil Pipelines Act Cap. 338
- Hydrocarbon Oil Refineries Act
- Petroleum Production and Distribution (Anti - Sabotage) Act No. 353
- Mineral Oils (Safety) Regulations
- Petroleum Regulations
- Petroleum Refining Regulations
- Crude Oil (Transportation and Shipment) Regulations
- Petroleum Products (Prices of Automotive Lubricating Oils) Order

- Petroleum Products (Uniform Retail Prices) Order
- Oil and Gas Pipelines Regulations 1995.

Transportation

Once the oil is produced, it is transported to refineries by pipelines and oil tankers. This is irrespective of whether the oil is being exported or being used domestically since the usefulness of oil only becomes apparent after it has been refined. The different products from the refinery are generally transported by pipelines and oil tankers, and, within the country, by road tankers. In Nigeria, rail transportation plays a negligible role because of the poor state of the railways.

Petroleum products are distributed within the country through a pipeline network of 4,000 - 5,000 kilometres interconnected between the nation's four refineries and 21 depots. This network is operated by the Petroleum Products Marketing Company Limited. In addition, marine tankers ferry products from the refineries to depots. Generally, movement of the products from the depots is by road.

The movement of petroleum products is the responsibility of the marketer. Through tankers, the products are conveyed to the service stations where they are retailed to the customer.

The Oil Pipelines Act, Cap. 338, and the Oil and Gas Pipelines Regulations 1995 both apply to products, S.11 (2) of the Oil Pipelines Act defines a pipeline as being:

> ...for the convenience of mineral oils, natural gas and any of their derivatives or components, and also any substance (including steam or water) used or intended to be used in the production or refining or conveying of mineral oils, natural gas, and any of their derivatives or components.

The Law and Regulations give detailed requirements, guidelines and standards for the grant of a permit to survey a pipeline route and for a licence to construct and operate a pipeline.

The application for a permit to survey should be addressed to the Minister and delivered to the Director of the Department of Petroleum Resources.[1] The applicant must undertake an environment impact assessment (EIA) study of the project, according to the Regulations. The Environmental Impact Assessment Act also requires full EIA for kilometres in excess of 50 kilometres and a partial EIA for lesser lengths. Both the Department and the Federal Environmental Protection Agency[2] have requirements that must be satisfied by the applicant.

The powers of a licence holder are quite extensive:[3]

(1) A licence shall entitle the holder, his officers, agents, workmen or other servants with any necessary equipment or vehicles, subject to the provisions of sections 14, 15 and 16 of this Act, to enter upon, take possession of or use a strip of land of a width not exceeding two hundred feet or of such other width or widths as may be specified in the licence upon the route specified in the licence, and thereon there over or thereunder to construct, maintain and operate oil pipeline and ancillary installations.

(2) For the purpose of this Act, an oil pipeline means a pipeline for the conveyance of mineral oils, natural gas and any of their derivatives or components, and also any

---

1 Parts II and III, Oil Pipelines Act Cap. 338, LFN 1990

2 On the status of the Federal Environmental Protection Agency see Topic XI below.

3 Ss.11 (1)-(4) Oil Pipelines Act.

substance (including steam and water) used or intended to be used in the production or refining or conveying of mineral oils, natural gas, and any of their derivatives or components.

(3) The power to construct, maintain and operate an oil pipeline shall include a power to construct, maintain and operate on the route of such pipeline all other installations (referred to in this Act as "ancillary installations") that are ancillary to the construction, maintenance and operation of such pipeline, including roadways, telephones and telegraph lines (subject to section 4 of the Telegraphs Act), electric power cables (subject to the provisions of the Electricity Act), pumping stations, storage tanks and loading terminals.

(4) The holder of a licence shall have power to dig and get free of charge any gravel, sand, clay, stone or other similar substance (not being a mineral within the meaning assigned thereto in the Mineral Act) within[4] any land included within the area covered by the licence to the extent that such gravel, sand, clay, stone or other substance, will facilitate the construction or maintenance of a pipeline or any ancillary installation.

A licence is for a maximum of 20 years. Upon expiration the holder must apply for a new licence and not a renewal.

The pipeline grid is currently stated to be at less than optimal levels, because of leakages and damaged pipelines. Some feel that the condition and efficiency of pipeline service will be enhanced if the private sector is more involved. Then, private companies would provide pipelines which could be

---

[4] For detailed procedure of the licensing process, see M.M. Olisa, *Nigerian Petroleum Law and Practice*, Chapter 4.

utilised by other persons. However the Nigerian law as it exists would have to be amended to allow for this. According to S.18(1) of the Oil Pipelines Act a person may use a pipeline not owned by him. The application is made to the Minister and he has the final say concerning the approval of this application. Such government power is unlikely to be readily accepted by a private company. In several developed countries third party access is accepted and accommodated under the respective municipal legal systems. In these countries the distribution networks function efficiently and the pipeline users have a choice as to which organisation they should utilise.

Refining

The Petroleum Refining Regulations, the 1993 Guidelines issued by the Minister and the Hydrocarbon Oil Refineries Act all regulate refining in Nigeria. A prospective refinery owner has to apply for a licence to construct or operate a refinery. This application must be accompanied by a detailed study of the project and a non-refundable fee. According to the Petroleum Refining (Amendment) Regulations 1996 the application fee is US $50,000 and US $100,000 for the issue of a refiner's licence.

The Regulations and Guidelines are quite detailed. The plant must conform to the approved inspections which will be undertaken. After permission to commission and operate the refinery has been given several conditions must be satisfied. These include the appointment of a qualified refinery manager, and a complete equipment report with evidence of availability of adequate spare parts. Any amendment or modification of the existing refinery also requires the minister's prior approval.

Presently there are four refineries in Nigeria, one in Warri, two in Port Harcourt and one in Kaduna. Cumulatively these refineries have a combined installed capacity of 445,000 barrels. This is stated to be above the estimated domestic consumption rate. However, for years the refineries have been functioning below capacity because they were not well maintained. As a result, the last few years of military rule were characterised by regular acute fuel shortages. The shortfall was initially met by a systematic schedule of product importation, geared at satisfying domestic consumption without any disruptions.[5] However this system was removed and replaced by unplanned and spasmodic importation of products which was markedly unsuccessful but which continued nonetheless because of the immense profits derived by the importers, who were well-connected to the regimes in power. The result of this system was that the last few years of military rule were characterised by regular acute shortages and long queues for petrol and kerosene. The situation eased slightly under the Abubakar administration, as a result of measures put in place. These measures included deregulation and a slight increase in product pricing, from ₦11.00 to ₦20.00 per litre.

Under the democratic regime the deregulation continues and apparently, there has been a dismantling of the patronage system of products importation. There has been a ten-percent increase in the price of petrol. Also maintenance of the refineries is a priority. The measures appear to have been

---

[5] See Jemine Akpieyi "Managing Domestic Fuel Scarcity. A Historical Perspective" in V.E. Eromosele (Ed), *Nigerian Petroleum Business: A Handbook*, Advent Communications Ltd 1997, 343 at 344 – 345.

somewhat successful as there have been fewer periods of scarcity since May 29, 1999.

Marketing

Section 4 of the Petroleum Act provides that no person shall store sell or distribute any petroleum products in Nigeria without a licence granted by the Minister. There are two exceptions to this law:

(1) Small quantities of 500 litres or less of kerosene and selected other products.
(2) Products that are not being stored in connection with importation, sale or distribution of petroleum products.

This provision appears to exclude exported products.

In Nigeria, NNPC sells products for domestic consumption through PPMC. Strangely, considering the fuel scarcity within the country, Nigeria exports many types of products such as automotive gas oil (AGO) low pour fuel oil (LPFO) and high pour fuel oil (HPFO). This was the case even when there was an acute shortage of these products within the country and they were selling for sums far in excess of their official prices.

PPMC sells to petroleum product marketing companies who are to conform to laid down guidelines for steady distribution and sale at uniform prices throughout the country. Dealers are paid a commission or margin for products lifted and sold. The uniform pricing system is funded from the Petroleum Equalisation Fund. This fund was established by the Petroleum Equalisation Fund (Management Board, etc.)

Act 1973. The Fund is for the reimbursement of oil marketing companies for any losses sustained as a result of the uniform pricing system. The money for the fund is apparently from "net surplus revenue recoverable from an oil marketing company." The current state of this fund is unclear.

This is because successive price hikes have reduced the marketers' margins. The margin of 28 kobo when the price of petrol/litre was 70 kobo was 40% of the pump price. When the price went to ₦3.25/litre the margin was 48 kobo or 14.8%. At the 1994 price, the marketers margin of ₦1.30/litre was 11.8%. Thus it can be seen that the margin has been consistently on the decline. Notwithstanding, reports indicate that the PEF is in fact quite robust. The source of these funds is not easily ascertainable. The fact that the Fund has been functional all this while seems to imply that surplus revenue existed under the rate of ₦11/litre which prevailed from 1994 to December 1998. Logically speaking, if a surplus exists, it means that the price in question must be adequate or even capable of being reduced if the government removes the uniform pricing system.

Petrochemicals

Petrochemicals are chemicals derived from hydrocarbons. There are numerous types. The basic components are produced by cracking naphtha and ethane. These components are the olefins, ethylene, propylene, butylenes, butadiene and the aromatics BTX. So many things can be made from petrochemicals e.g. drugs, tyres, synthetic fabrics, disposable nappies, sweeteners, etc. It is true to say that petrochemicals are an indispensable part of modern life.

In Nigeria petrochemicals are produced at the Warri Refinery, the Kaduna refinery and Eleme Petrochemicals Complex near Port Harcourt Rivers State.

The production capacity of these plants is as follows:

Product	*Maximum Capacity*
tonnes/year	
Polypropylene	35,000
Carbon black	18,000
Linear alkyl benzene	30,000
Kero solvent	38,000
Benzene	15,000
Ethylene	260,000
Propylene	90,000
Butene-1	22,000
Polyethylene (LLD/HD)	250,000
Polypropylene	80,000

These products can be used for the manufacture of items such as detergents, lubricants, insecticides, woven sacks, bottle crates, tyres and tubes.

In the early 1980s the government saw the petrochemicals industry as a core economic project that would diversify foreign exchange earnings and reduce importation. It therefore embarked upon the creation of this industry, initially in two phases. Phase I, initially put at $500 million and consisting of the plants at Ekpan (near Warri) and Kaduna, was commissioned in 1988 after a delay of three years.

The table above covers what is currently in operation, Phase I and Stage one of Phase II, that is, the Eleme Plant, which is mainly for olefins.

Phase I suffered from two major shortcomings[6]. First of all, the production of polypropylene fell far short of domestic demand and therefore, the domestic production made little impact. Secondly, since the operations of Phase I were dependent on refinery feedstock, it was essential for the Warri and Kaduna refineries to function efficiently and at capacity. However the past few years have been characterised by under - producing refineries that are inadequately maintained.

The Eleme Petrochemicals Complex (EPC) is based on feedstock extracted from natural gas liquids (NGL) from nearby gas fields. Phase II remains uncompleted. Stages two and three of Phase II are still on the drawing board as is Phase III. Phase III would produce advanced aromatic intermediates such as benzene, tuolene, phenol, polystyrene, etc. These can be used by the building, automotive, agricultural, electrical industries. Feedstock for this complex will be from the, refineries and the Phases I and II plants. It is hoped that Phase III will actually end up being completed. Currently the legal framework on petrochemicals is sparse. It would appear that the "Guidelines for the Establishment of a Petroleum Refinery, Petrochemical and Gas Processing Plant in Nigeria," issued by the Minister under Regs. 2 and 23 of the Petroleum Refining Regulations is the main regulatory document. It should be noted that the definition of refining within these Regulations encompasses petrochemical plants.

> 'refining' includes the liquefying of petroleum gas or gases by whatever method, separating crude oil by whatever method into any grade of petroleum product, treating and upgrading of any petroleum or petroleum

[6] See Sarah A. Khan, *Nigeria: The Political Economy of Oil*, Oxford University Press, 1994, at Chap. 6

> products by whatever method into other product or products.

This definition validly covers petrochemical plants as they are 'for the treating and upgrading of any petroleum products by whatever method into other product or products.'

Selected reading materials

M. M. Olisa, *Nigeria Petroleum Law and Practice*, Chapter 4

Various articles in V.E. Eromosele, *Nigeria Petroleum Business: A Handbook*, Advent Publications, 1998.

Topic X

Trade in crude oil and products

Crude oil is probably the most important traded commodity in the world because of its use as a source of energy and because it is so versatile. Also, its importance arises from the fact that the major consumers are different from the major exporting countries and therefore large volumes are traded across national boundaries.

Historical perspective of crude oil trade

From the inception of the oil industry until the end of the 1960s the international oil industry was dominated by the major oil companies, who controlled the concessions in the producing countries. These companies tended to act in concert and therefore the market remained very stable. Prices were set by the companies without consulting the host countries. OPEC was in fact created in reaction to the unilateral reduction of posted prices by the major oil companies.

When OPEC was formed, it's first concern, in accordance with its stated aims, was to stabilise oil prices. In doing this it encouraged members to regain ownership over their petroleum resources and to attempt to control their internal oil industries.

This led to OPEC gaining *de facto* control over internationally traded oil, to the extent that, by the early 1970s it determined the fixed price and differentials for all the crudes produced by the member states. It was able to do this because, at that time, it controlled the greater percentage of internationally traded crude. As a result the price of oil rose dramatically, rising to over $40 in the early 1970s.

OPEC set up a pricing structure with the following objectives:

- To stabilise the market through the establishment of an official selling price.
- To set prices for the different crudes produced by the member countries, taking into account the difference in crude quality and freight cost, and the volume available for sale.

Initially spot transactions were few. With time they became increasingly acceptable as the spot price was simply the price that a buyer was willing to pay a seller. It could be either higher or lower than the official selling price (OSP). It was only a matter of time before the spot price would compete seriously against the OSP regime, undermine its position in world oil trade, and eventually become the more important pricing mechanism.

OPEC's influence was also undermined by the creation of the International Energy Agency (IEA) in 1973. The IEA was formed by the Western consuming nations to counter the dominance of OPEC. These countries, *inter alia*, adopted policies to encourage exploration in non-OPEC countries, and to maximise the use of oil through conservation of use. Again, a lot of measures were put in place by the developed countries to discourage states from joining OPEC. As a result of these and other measures, by the mid-1980s OPEC had ceased to control crude oil trade and the price had started slipping. In a bid to control this downward trend, OPEC introduced the quota system, which set ceilings of production for each member country, based on production capacity and on financial needs. This system remains until today. However the oil price is no longer controlled by OPEC as several non-OPEC producers and exporters abound.[1] The oil price is now completely subject to market forces of supply and demand. It is also prone to serious fluctuations. 1986 was memorable for serious price reversals from $25/barrel at the beginning of the year, to less than $10/barrel by August 1986. From 1999 prices have been rising steadily. Whilst the late 1980s to late 1990s were characterised by prices between the range of $15-$18, since 1999 prices have gone as high as $34, notwithstanding increased production by OPEC members.

Crude oil contracts

Crude oil is traded either under a term contract for a fixed period of time or under isolated or spot transactions. Nigerian crude allocated to NNPC is normally sold through term contracts. The same holds true for most of the volumes accruing to the joint venture partners or contractors, which are often sent to subsidiary refinery companies. However the spot market is very significant and therefore merits some separate consideration.

---

[1] E.g. Russia, Great Britain, Norway, Mexico, who are all amongst the world's major exporters. *Source*: http://www.iea.org, the website of the International Energy Agency.

The term contract

The conditions for Nigerian term contracts are set by NNPC from time to time. These guidelines have remained substantially the same over the years. However, they have not often been followed and many legal persons who did not meet the criteria were given allocations during the past military regimes. From July 1999 the following conditions must be met by a prospective buyer.

A prospective applicant must be:

- a *bona fide* end user who owns a refinery and retail outlets abroad. Details of the applicant's facilities markets and volumes of crude oil processed over the last three years must accompany the applicant, or,
- an established and globally recognised large volume trader. The applicant must provide evidence of its global network, its activities and volume of crude oil handled in the last three years; or
- a company that has built an export oil refinery in Nigeria.

Any applicant must have a minimum annual turnover of at least $100 million and a network of at least $40 million. Also the successful applicant must show commitment to the development of the Nigerian economy by investing in the oil industry or other sectors. Alternatively the applicant may make 'meaningful and sizeable' investments in community development projects in the oil producing communities.

The Guidelines issued by the NNPC give the following examples of investment areas;

- Upstream investments to increase oil reserves and production capacity.
- Downstream projects in refining, processing, distribution and storage of petroleum products.

- Gas utilisation projects.
- Solid mineral development.
- Industries with foreign exchange earning potential (and any other area acceptable to the seller).

Also, successful companies are required to post a $1 million performance bond which will be cashed after six months of the signing of the crude oil contract, if no investment has been made "or there is no evidence of a commitment to do so". In addition to the forfeiture of the bond the contract will automatically terminate. Lifting shall be on the basis of a confirmed irrevocable letter of credit in the name of the holder.

Candidates will be shortlisted if the NNPC receives positive economic intelligence reports that confirm the applicant's capacity to apply, and financial status. According to the Guidelines the government shall endeavour to maintain regional balance in the distribution of Nigerian crude oil contract holdings. For this purpose the regions are; North and South America, Western Europe/Mediterranean, Former Soviet Union and Eastern Europe, Asia and Australia, and Africa.

From the list of successful applicants commencing October 1999, the above criteria appeared to have been adhered to. See table below.[2]

List of successful applicants

1. Republic of South Africa	55,000 barrels
2. National Oil Corporation of Kenya	30,000 barrels
3. Ghana National Oil Corporation	30,000 barrels

[2] *This Day*, Tuesday August 17, 1999, Front page.

4. North Atlantic Refinery of Canada	50,000	barrels
5.Kyokuto Petroleum Ind. Of Tokyo	100,000	barrels
6. Addax Nigeria Limited (Swiss)	90,000	barrels
7. Glencore International AG	90,000	barrels
8. Total International Firm	50,000	barrels
9. Attock Oil International	60,000	barrels
10. Vitol SA	60,000	barrels
11. Trafigura Beheer, Amsterdam	60,000	barrels
12. Arcadia, London	100,000	barrels
13. Itochu, Japan	20,000	barrels
14. Carbon of Bermuda	30,000	barrels
15. Duke Oil Services	20,000	barrels
16. Napoil Limited	20,000	barrels
	---------	--------
TOTAL	865,000	barrels

Of this list, the first three are arrangements with African governments whilst the last three have ongoing contractual relationships with NNPC. The fourth to thirteenth are established crude oil traders, from America, Europe or the Far East.

Spot and forward markets

Crude oil and products are often sold in the spot, or forward market.

The spot market for crude

The term 'spot market' refers to isolated product sales, which may be immediately available, or in few weeks time.

The spot market has no physical location and is open to any one with a phone, means of electronic communication, and the financial capacity. Main operators in the international spot markets are:

- International oil companies
- National oil companies of producing countries
- Oil traders who may be independent companies or a trading subsidiary of one of the international oil companies.

There are a few major markets for crude, each of which tends to concentrate on particular types of crude, such as Brent or West Texas Intermediate. For products, the Rotterdam market is well known. In this instance the market is so named because the product vessels often berth at or around Rotterdam. Major cities of the world, such as New York, London and Singapore feature prominently because of the large concentration of traders in these areas.

A well known example of a spot market is the *Brent Market* which is the spot market for a blend of North Sea crudes which are shipped from the Sullom Voe terminal on the Shetland Islands, Scotland. Brent blend is very similar to Arabian Light, West Texas Intermediate, Bonny and Forcados[3] crudes, and can be substituted for any of them.

The spot market can be a straightforward sale of a specific cargo, to be available within a specific date range at a price agreed at the time of contract. Alternatively it could be a forward transaction, which refers to an agreement to sell or buy a cargo for delivery on an unspecified day of a given month. "15 day Brent" is an example of a complex forward transaction. It is the purchase of a claim on a cargo of Brent at a future period, normally 3-4 months ahead. Between the first

---

[3] Bonny and Forcados are Nigerian crudes.

transaction and the date of delivery, the cargo changes hands several times, sometime up to a few dozen times. These numerous transactions are called *Daisy Chains*. The Brent market is very volatile and has collapsed in the past due to extremely long daisy chains and the inabilities of some involved parties to honour their obligations.

Trade in products in Nigeria

Petroleum products are defined in S.15 of the Petroleum Act. Presently, this trade is regulated and controlled by the government. The main enactment in this area is the Petroleum Regulations. This law lays down rules for the storage and transportation of petroleum and for LPG (liquefied petroleum gas).

Bunkering

This term is familiar to the average Nigerian and colloquially denotes illegal petroleum trading. A bunker fuel is one which is used for ship engines. Bunkering refers to trade in these fuels, usually to the vessel that is using the fuel (to "bunker" is to fuel a ship), and it is not an illegal trade per se. Any illegality arises when a company that does not have a license engages in bunkering. Normally, the licensees are to be found amongst the major marketers, marketers, and these licenses are granted to companies who have satisfied conditions stipulated by the Ministry of Petroleum Resources.

Under the Special Tribunal (Miscellaneous Offences) Act Cap. 410,[4] any person who deals in petroleum products without a license is liable on conviction, to imprisonment for life. In addition any vehicle, vessel, aircraft or other conveyance used shall be forfeited to the Federal Government.

Selected reading materials

Published African and Nigerian articles in this are apparently few.

M. M. Olisa, at Chapter 7

Blanche Sas "Legal Aspects of the 15 day Brent Market," Part 1, Vol. 5, No. 2 1987 *JERL* 109.

Current information on Nigerian trade and trading patterns can be obtained from editions of *Nigeria's Oil and Gas Monthly.*

[4] Sec. 17.

Topic XI

Environmental issues

Environmental issues are now of paramount importance and the oil industry is, directly and indirectly, at the centre of the current problem. Research in the latter half of the twentieth century has discovered that industrial processes have changed the earth in many fundamental ways. The seas are polluted to the detriment of various marine flora and fauna; the desert is expanding; the ozone layer is getting damaged, the global climate is being altered; and there is a rapid extinction of plant and animal species.

Hydrocarbons have the capacity to pollute the land, seas and atmosphere greatly. Also the industry is a major culprit in the depletion of the ozone layer.

Types of pollution

Environmental pollution has been simply defined as the addition to the natural environment of any substance or energy form (e.g. heat, sound) at a rate that results in higher than natural concentrations of that substance, and therefore has an adverse effect. The actions of pollutants vary greatly. Noise pollution is localized and its effects are short-lived i.e. for as long as the noise exists. Conversely some types of pollutants disperse very readily, are world-wide in distribution, and their effects are permanent. In this group we find the carbon based emissions of the oil industry that are a bye product of major industrial activity, which are said to form 60% of the carbon dioxide emissions world-wide and which have led to the greenhouse effect.

Greenhouse gases, climate change and the ozone layer

There are certain gases in the atmosphere, which are called *greenhouse gases* because they form a blanket around the earth that warms it up. Without this blanket it is estimated that the earth's surface would be 30^{0c} colder than it is today. Key greenhouse gases are carbon dioxide (CO_2); methane (CH_4); nitrous oxide (N_2O) and chlorofluorocarbons (CFC). This blanket is known as the *ozone layer*. As a result of industrial activity since the Industrial Revolution in England in the eighteenth century, this blanket has been getting progressively thicker. Also increased industrial activity has resulted in deforestation. When forests are cut down the carbon stored in the trees escapes to the atmosphere. When cattle are raised or rice is planted, gases such as methane and nitrous oxide are emitted. To give other examples when coal, oil and natural gas are burnt or utilised for powering engines and cars, large amounts of carbon dioxide are spewed into the air.

The thickening of the ozone layer means that there is likely to be increased global warming of 1 to 3.5oC over the next one hundred years. What this means in practical terms is uncertain because the global climate is rather complicated. Sea levels are predicted to rise, threatening low coastal areas near sea level. It is estimated that there will be changes in rainfall and wind patterns. There could also be floods and famine and other catastrophes. What is certain is that climatic conditions have changed in many areas world-wide. Even now the average person in Nigeria is almost certain that seasons are hotter than they have been for sometime, and that they have become quite unpredictable.

It must be stated that there is not total agreement amongst experts concerning the effects of these environmental changes.[1] However, the enormity of possible consequences of climate change means that all should take measures that will not cause further damage. This perspective is captured in the following quote:[2]

> If someone shouts 'LION' in the dark you would be foolish indeed to sit still and relax just because you cannot tell which direction the beast is coming from. But how far would you run for fear of the lion? Naturally, you would run until dawn, when it should be clear that the lion really exists.

International conventions on the environment

Environmental issues are of international importance as invariably, negative effects of harmful practices cannot easily be limited and/or contained within national boundaries. Therefore there are several international conventions, declarations and resolutions such as the following:

- Declaration of the United Nations Conference on the Human Environment (Stockholm, 16 June 1972)

---

[1] See the OPEC perspective in "OPEC's view on climate change" at their website, htt://www.opec.org.

[2] Shakespeare Maya, "Viewpoint: Lion in the Dark", *Climate Change*, November 1997.

- UN General Assembly Resolution 37/7 and Annex: World Charter for Nature (28 October 1982).
- The Rio Declaration on Environment and Development (Rio de Janeiro, 13 June 1992).
- Instrument for the Establishment of the Restructured Global Environment Facility (GEF) (Geneva, 16 March 1994).
- Vienna Convention for the Protection of the Ozone Layer (Vienna, 22 March 1985).
- Montreal Protocol on Substances that deplete the Ozone Layer 1987 (Amended London 27 – 29 June 1990; Nairobi 19-21 June 1991; Copenhagen 23-25 November 1992).
- UN Framework Convention on Climate Change (New York, 9 May 1992)
- The Kyoto Protocol to the UN Framework Convention on Climate Change. (Kyoto, December 1997).
- Convention on International Trade in Endangered Species of Wild Fauna and Flora (CITES) (Washington, 3 March 1973).
- Convention on Biological Diversity (Rio de Janeiro, 5 June 1992.
- Non-legally Binding Authorisation Statement of Principles for a Global Consensus on the Management, Conservation and Sustainable Development of all types of Forest (Rio de Janeiro, 13 June 1992)
- International Tropical Timber Agreement (Geneva, 21 January 1994)
- Basel Convention on the Control of Trans-boundary Movements of Hazardous Wastes and their Disposal (Basel, 22 March 1989).

- Convention on Third Party Liability in the Field of Nuclear Energy (Paris, 29 July 1960) and Supplementary Convention (Brussels 31 January 1963).
- International Convention on Civil Liability for Oil Pollution Damage (Brussels 29 November 1969) and Protocol (London, 19 November 1976).
- International Convention on the Establishment of an International Fund for Compensation for Oil Pollution Damage (Brussels, 18 December 1971).

The 1992 United Nations Framework Convention on Climate Change

The United Nations Framework Convention on Climate Change was signed at Rio de Janeiro. Fifty ratifications were needed for it to come into force. This was achieved by December 1993 and the Convention entered into force on 21st March 1994. As at April 1998, 165 states had ratified the convention.

Under the Climate Change Convention, parties agree to take precautionary measures to mitigate causes and anticipate impacts of climate change. In doing this the treaty promotes a new international principle called the 'precautionary principle', under which activities which threaten to cause serious or irreversible damage can be restricted or even prohibited before there is absolute scientific certainty about their effects.

The parties agree to take climate change into account in such matters as agriculture, energy, natural resources, and activities involving the sea- coast. They agree to co-operate to reduce greenhouse gas emissions to 1990 levels by the year 2000.

The convention provides for the use of protocols for specific measures. In 1997, at Kyoto, a Protocol known as the Kyoto Protocol has set targets and timetables for the control of greenhouse gas emission. This Protocol is yet to come into force. For some developed countries, notably the United States, the problem is that while obligations as to the reduction of emissions are imposed on the industrialised countries, there are no corresponding obligations for developing countries. Presently that makes ratification by the United States unlikely and jeopardises the international attempts at controlling emissions.

Lead poisoning

Lead is a soft, silvery - white or greyish metal. It is highly durable and resistant to corrosion, qualities which make it widely used in chemical and other industries. A lead compound, tetraethyl lead (TEL) is added to petrol to boost its octane number and thereby to improve its quality. Lead is however a toxic element which is retained in the body when ingested. It accumulates in a body until a lethal quantity is reached when it can cause different illnesses in adults and particularly, children. Children are more susceptible to lead poisoning from petrol because they are nearer street level and to the exhaust pipes, which spew out the lead in the fuel. Symptoms of lead poisoning include fatigue, respiratory disorder, eye irritation, nausea, irritability, cardinal disorders, hypertension, neuro-psychological effects and other behavioural impairments.

Lead does not have to be added to petrol, and in some countries it is not. However, Nigerian refineries are said to produce only leaded fuels. In Nigeria the lead limit is 0.7g Pb/l which is regarded as high. National fuel consumption is estimated to be 20 million litres a day, which means that 15,000 kilograms of lead are emitted into the environment every day just through the burning of fuels.[3] While lead contamination can be from other sources such as paint and insecticides, petrol is said to be the source of 80 - 90 percent of all environmental lead contamination. A 1991 study of roadside dust samples showed more than 6,000 parts per million of lead on Lagos sheets. This is frightening when one considers that in the United States paint or paint work at less than 600 parts per million is considered hazardous to children.

Lead poisoning endangers future generations and the nation. The only solutions are however municipal. Unlike the greenhouses gases, deleterious effects of lead are localised because it is a solid. It is possible for leaded fuel to be banned, for the refineries to produce only lead free petrol and for only lead free petrol to be imported. This can be done through appropriate legislation and monitoring mechanisms.[4]

Oil industry pollution in Nigeria

Petroleum operations give rise to various types of pollution at any stage from the processes of exploration and production, to when the refined products are being transported and utilised. The types of pollution could be air, water, land, noise, or thermal pollution. One industrial activity can give rise to several types of pollution. For example, gas flaring is

---

[3] Assuming, of course, that the refineries are fully functioning.

[4] Sam Agbo, "Effects of Lead poisoning in Children," in A.A. Falomo and C.C. Chikwendu (Eds)_*Proceedings of a Workshop on Vehicular Emission and Lead Poisoning in Nigeria*, Friends of the Environment (FOTE), Lagos, 1998, p.20 at 21.

extremely deleterious to the environment and causes thermal, noise, air, land and water pollution.

Oil spillage

Spillages can occur at any stage in oil industry operations. Crude and refined oil are both pollutants that have lasting and deleterious effects on the environment. While the big disasters get a lot of attention, small-scale pollution occurs all the time all over the country, without being noticed. For example few people realise, when they ask the petrol attendants to fill their cars to the brim, and the overflow spills onto the ground, that they are in fact contributing to the degradation of the environment. Those "little drops" that are spilled every time a fuel tank is filled, add up to a sizeable amount of wasted petrol. A second common and overlooked example is to be found in the typical mechanic shop, where used engine oil is carelessly thrown away, in ignorance of the fact that used oil is a hazardous waste which contains toxic materials, does great harm to the environment, and can even be carcinogenic.

Causes of crude oil spills have been classified as being equipment failure, sabotage, human error, corrosion, blow-outs, engineering errors, natural causes, acts of third parties, erosion, and accidents. Data show that most spills are attributable to technical reasons such as corrosion or equipment failure. A number of spills are attributable to sabotage which is defined as a wilful attempt to disrupt or interrupt the production or distribution of oil by third parties. Sabotage is a result of poverty and ignorance. Often members of the community where oil is being produced tamper with oil installations so that their property will be damaged and compensation will be paid to them. It is now a crime with very stiff penalties.[5] The law also provides that no compensation is payable for a spill attributable to sabotage. However, the final way of solving the problem of sabotage probably lies in educating the people as to the adverse effects of oil pollution, and also in the Government and companies jointly working to ensure that the oil producing communities are provided with a few basic amenities (see topic XII below).

The legal regulation of the Nigerian oil industry

Several laws regulate the activities of the oil industry vis-à-vis the environment. These include:

- The Petroleum Act, Cap 350, LFN 1990 and its attendant regulations.
- The Oil in Navigable Waters Act Cap 331, LFN 1990 and its attendant regulations.
- The Oil Terminal Dues Act, Cap 339, LFN 1990.
- The Associated Gas Re-Injection Act Cap 26 LFN 1990, and its attendant regulations.
- The Federal Environment Protection Agency Act Cap. 131 LFN 1990.

The Petroleum Act generally empowers the Minister in Section 9-(1) (b) (iii) to make regulations for the prevention of pollution of watercourses and the atmosphere. Accordingly the Petroleum Regulations 1969 contain provisions on environmental pollution. There is an 'omnibus' provision on pollution in Regulation 25, which provides that:

> The licensee or lessee shall adopt all practicable precautions including the provision of up-to-date equipment approved by the Director of Petroleum

[5] See the Petroleum Production and Distribution (Anti-Sabotage) Act, Cap. 353, Laws of the Federation of Nigeria.

> Resources to prevent pollution of inland waters, rivers, water courses, the territorial waters of Nigeria or the high seas by oil, mud or other fluid or substances which might contaminate the water, bank or shore line which might cause harm or destruction to fresh water or marine life and where any such pollution occurs or has occurred, shall take prompt steps to control and, if possible, end it.

This provision suffers from two major defects. First of all, a rather vague legal duty is imposed, as all the operator is enjoined to do is to take prompt steps 'to control and, if possible, end' the pollution in question. Secondly it does not deal with land pollution at all.

Regulation 36 enjoins the operator to carry out his operations in accordance with good oil field practices, and to take "reasonable steps" to control the flow and prevent the escape of waste out from relevant areas. Regulations 38 and 39 provide for the use of approved methods and practices for the production of oil and gas and for confirming petroleum respectively. These and similar regulations are not very stringent and are loosely worded. In addition, they contain only an unrealistic and unlikely penalty of revocation if they are contravened by an operator.

The Petroleum Regulations 1967 deal with downstream activities of the petroleum industry and contain provisions against the leakage of petroleum products. Penalties for non-compliance are revocation, and a fine of ₦100 with the option of imprisonment. The Petroleum Refining Regulations 1974 also, amongst other things, deal with environmental standards applicable in Nigerian refineries. Regulation 43, for example, deals with effluent and drainage disposal and imposes a duty on the Manager to ensure that disposal is in accordance with good refining practices.[6] The Manager is also obliged to prevent pollution and "where it occurs, take prompt steps to control, and if possible, end it."[7] Again, an officer found guilty under this Provision is liable to a fine of ₦100 or imprisonment. The penalties for contraventions are not really feasible in practice. Revocation is unrealistic and unlikely to be utilised unless it is a major environmental offence. A fine of ₦100 is laughable, can deter only the very poor members of the population, and certainly not an oil corporation. The prison term is impracticable for corporate offenders.

It should be noted that the low legal obligations imposed by these provisions place a greater responsibility on the Department of Petroleum Resources to define and delimit the scope of terms such as "good oilfield practice", and approved methods and practices.

The Federal Environmental Protection Agency Act

This law was enacted in 1988, after a long gestation period of 12 years. It is the first Nigerian statute to deal exclusively with the environment. The Act establishes the Federal Environmental Protection Agency, which is to be responsible for the protection of the Nigerian environment. The Agency is to advise the Government on environmental matters and to design periodic master plans for the development of environmental science and technology. In performing its functions it is to work in co-operation with state ministries, Local Government Councils and statutory bodies.

The Agency is responsible for the establishment of national environmental standards, and this could really be said

---

[6] Reg. 43(1)
[7] Reg. 43(3)

to be its major function. Penalties are specified for the discharge of hazardous substances constituting harmful waste into the land, water or air. These are ₦100,000 for individuals and ₦500,000 for corporate offenders. Hazardous wastes are defined under the Harmful Waste (Special Criminal Provisions) Act 1988 as:

> any injurious, poisonous, toxic, noxious substance and in particular nuclear waste emitting any radio-active substance if the waste is in such quantity, whether with any other consignment of the same for different substances as to subject any person to the risk of death, fatal injury or incurable impairment of physical or mental health.[8]

By this definition, oil is a hazardous substance, and therefore comes under the orbit of the sections which prohibit the discharge of such substances.

In the exercise of its powers and functions FEPA has instituted a number of Regulations; Guidelines and other rules aimed at controlling pollution and protecting the environment. Some notable ones are:

- the National Policy on the Environment, 1989 – which aims to provide a rational, practicable, coherent, comprehensive and sustainable approach to the pursuit of economic and social development. It sets policy goals, provides the concepts and stipulates the strategies which will lead to the procedures, and other concrete actions required for launching the country into an era of sustainable development.
- *Guidelines and Standards for Environmental Pollution Control in Nigeria, 1991*- which direct industries to

[8] S. 15

improve the quality of the environment and free it from pollutants and other environmental hazards. They serve, more or less, as recommended standards of environmentally good behaviour for industries.

- The *National Environmental Protection (Effluent Limitations) Regulations, 1991* – which enjoin every industry to, among others things, install anti-pollution equipment for detoxification of its affluent and chemical discharges and treat the same to stipulated levels before discharging.
- The *National Environmental Protection (Pollution Abatement in Industries and Facilities Generating Wastes) Regulations, 1991* – which prohibit the release of hazardous or toxic substances into the environment beyond the limits approved by the Agency and provides for other requirements and procedures e.g. in cases of accidental or unusual discharges, and also require industries to obtain permits for discharges that are beyond permissible limits.
- *Waste Management and Hazardous Waste Regulations, 1991* – which regulate the collection, treatment and disposal of solid and hazardous wastes from municipal and industrial sources, and provide a comprehensive list of chemicals and chemical wastes by toxicity categories.

Presently, the fate of FEPA is uncertain. Under restructuring that was done in late 1999 it appears that it will now be a department of the Ministry of the Environment and not a separate parastatal. It should be noted that the law establishing FEPA still stands and therefore, the restructuring, strictly speaking, has no legal basis. As at the time of writing, a draft Nigerian Environment Protection Act has been presented to the National Assembly. It is more comprehensive and detailed than the FEPA Act and it gives primary responsibility over the environment to the Federal Ministry of Environment. However, this initial draft does not repeal the FEPA Act.

Environmental Impact Assessment Decree 1992

The Environmental Impact Assessment Decree requires the government, its agencies, and private enterprises to take several significant steps before engaging in projects that may have environmental repercussions, from initial planning to implementation and afterwards.

One of such steps is to compulsorily make, in projects which may significantly affect the quality of the environment, a detailed assessment concerning the environmental impact of the project. This assessment will include adverse impacts that cannot be avoided, alternatives to the proposed action, cumulative, long and short-term effects, identification of measures available to mitigate adverse effects and an indication of cross-border effects. The law requires the publication of such assessment to enable interested parties to examine the environmental propriety and, if need be, object to the proposed project or activity before its commencement. It also stipulates various penalties for non-compliance and incorporates in its schedule a list of activities or projects for which environmental impact assessment is mandatory.

The Harmful Wastes (Special Criminal Provisions) Decree 1988

This was enacted in the wake of an incident when some Italian companies, with the collaboration of some local officials and citizens, imported and deposited some highly toxic and radioactive waste materials on a farmland near the local port at Koko town in Delta State. The Decree creates criminal offences in respect of movement handling and disposal of toxic and generally harmful substances on any land or territorial waters or contiguous zone, or Exclusive Economic Zone of Nigeria. It stipulates very stiff penalties.

Supervision and monitoring

The supervision and monitoring of the oil industry is the main responsibility of the Department of Petroleum Resources (DPR) of the Federal Ministry of Petroleum Resources. No law directly empowers DPR to undertake these functions. The NNPC Act specifically gives powers of regulation to the Petroleum Inspectorate, which is the precursor of DPR.

FEPA has over all responsibility for the Nigerian environment and thus, over the oil industry. In practice, this has led to problems of jurisdiction between the two bodies, and to the oil companies having to comply with two sets of regulations from two different agencies. As a result, the Environmental Unit of the Department of Petroleum Resources has been moved to be under FEPA. There is some resistance presently and one is uncertain of the final outcome. Even if the FEPA Act is repealed and its functions taken over by the Ministry of Environment, it is necessary to clarify and define the roles of the bodies responsible for the Nigerian environment, in such a way as to minimise conflicts.

Selected reading materials

M. T. Okorodudu-Fubara, *Law of Environmental Protection*, Caltop Publications (Nig) Ltd, 1998, especially chapter 6.

Various articles in the following publications:

- J. O. Omotola (Ed), *Environmental Law in Nigeria Including Compensation*
- F. Shyllon (Ed), *The Law and the Environment in Nigeria.* Faculty of Law, University of Ibadan.
- M. A. Ajomo, O. Adewale, *Environmental Law and Sustainable Development in Nigeria*, 1994 Nigeria Institute of Advanced Legal Studies, British Council.
- *The Petroleum Industry and the Nigerian Environment*, 1983, 1985 and 1987
- Subsequent publications of proceedings of the Biennial Seminar on the Petroleum Industry and the Nigerian Environment organised by the Department of Petroleum Resources.

Topic XII

Oil community issues

This topic deals with the rights of individuals and communities over the natural resources on and within their land, and the legal protection afforded them against the environmental ravages of petroleum exploration and production. This is particularly pertinent as for some years the oil communities have been quite militant in demanding their rights. It is important to acknowledge years of neglect and apathy on the part of the federal and state governments, which are partially responsible for an abysmal level of poverty and underdevelopment that is incomprehensible to those from other parts of Nigeria. These governments have a partial, and not total responsibility, for the underdevelopment in these areas because riverine communities in delta areas tend to be backward in development vis-à-vis other parts of the particular country within which they are situated because of their relative inaccessibility and the higher costs of development projects (for natural reasons such as the type of soil, higher technology, distance, etc.).

Nigeria's oil is mainly produced from the Niger Delta area, eighty per cent of which is located in Delta, Rivers and Bayelsa States. These three states produce 75% of the nations petroleum. Other states within which the Delta is situated are Edo, Cross River, Akwa Ibom and Ondo States.

The Niger Delta covers over 20,000 square kilometres, and is one of the largest deltas in the world. The people of the Niger Delta are primarily from the minority tribes of Nigeria and are very poor. They lack modern infrastructure and live under poor health conditions.

The oil communities are those located in the actual areas of exploration and production. For these communities the main legal issues are threefold:

- the right to development
- rights over natural resources
- rights for injuries suffered as a result of oil industry activities

The right to development

It is now internationally recognised that states have a right to development,[1] and a new branch of international law, known as international development law, has emerged. The 1986 United Nations General Assembly Declaration on the Right to Development[2] states that the right to development is an inalienable human right applicable to 'every human person and all peoples.' It further states that[3] 'the human person is the central subject of development and should be the active participant and beneficiary of development.' It also categorically gives states the right and the duty to formulate appropriate national development policies that aim at the

[1] However, some notable scholars still dispute the validity of this right. For readings on this see *Henry J. Steiner. Philip Alston, International Human Rights in Context: Law, Politics, Morals,* Clarendon Press, Oxford 1996, 1110 – 1146.

[2] General Assembly Resolution 41/128 of 1986

[3] Article 1.

constant improvement of the well-being of the entire population and of individuals, on the basis of their active, free and meaningful participation in development and in the fair distribution of the benefits therefrom.[4] Also 'states have the primary responsibility for the creation of national and international conditions favourable to the realisation of the right to development'.

It must always be borne in mind that General Assembly resolutions are not international legislation *per se,*[5] but at most evidence of the existence of international customary law. However, declarations and state practice, often within United Nations fora[6] have led to the emergence of this right for states and for people who are recognised as the subjects of development.

In Africa, the right of peoples to development is an international law. For states, such as Nigeria, that have enacted the African Charter of Human and Peoples' Rights as part of their national legislation, it is also a part of municipal law.

The African Charter is Cap. 7 of the Laws of the Federation of Nigeria 1990, and Article 22 states that:

- All peoples shall have the right to their economic, social and cultural development with due regard to their freedom and identity and in the equal enjoyment of the common heritage of mankind.
- States shall have the duty, individually or collectively, to ensure the exercise of the right to development.

---

[4] Article 2

[5] Any good international law textbook clearly deals with this when discussing 'Sources of International Law.'

[6] Peter Slinn, "The contribution of the United Nations to the Evolution of the Principles of International Development Law." ASICL Proc. 7 (1995), 263.

All major human rights instruments clearly speak of equality before the law.[7] The African Charter speaks of equality of peoples' and declares that:[8]

> All peoples shall be equal; they shall enjoy the same respect and shall have the same rights. Nothing shall justify the domination of a people by another.

Therefore there is a right to development for peoples; a right which surely applies to the oil producing communities and to any other communities in Nigeria.

Rights over natural resources

Some communities in the Niger Delta have attempted to assert rights over the natural resources under their land, notwithstanding the fact that sec 44(3) of the 1999 Constitution and section 1 of the Petroleum Act 1969, clearly vest ownership in the Federal Government.

It must be said that there are indigenous people's rights under international law and some feel that the oil communities are indigenous people and therefore that rights of such people belong to them. However a dictionary meaning of a word must be distinguished from its legal meaning. In a dictionary sense, indigenous people are those who can claim to be the original

---

[7] E.g. Preamble, Charter of the United Nations; Arts 1,1,6,7. Universal Declaration of Human Rights; Art. 3, International Covenant on Civil and Political Rights; Art. 3, 9,25, International Covenant on Economic, Social and Cultural Rights,

[8] In Article 19.

land owners, who have been living on and claiming ownership of the land in question "since time immemorial". The legal concept of indigenous people is defined in the International Labour Organisation Convention Concerning Indigenous and Tribal Peoples in Independent Countries 1989, which applies to:[9]

- tribal peoples in independent countries whose social, cultural and economic conditions distinguish them from other sections of the national community, and whose status is regulated wholly or partially by their own customs or traditions or by special laws or regulations.
- peoples in independent countries who are regarded as indigenous on account of their descent from the populations which inhabited the country, or a geographical region to which the country belongs, at the time of conquest or colonisation or the establishment of present state boundaries and who, irrespective of their legal status, retain some or all of their own social, economic, cultural and political institutions.
- Self-identification as indigenous or tribal shall be regarded as a fundamental criterion for determining the groups to which the provisions of this Convention apply.

A Guide to this Convention published by the ILO states that:[10]

> The term 'indigenous' refers to those who, while retaining totally or partially their traditional languages, institutions and lifestyles which distinguish them from

---

[9] Article 1.

[10] M. Tomei, L. Swepston, *Indigenous and Tribal Peoples: A Guide to ILO Convention No. 169*, ILO, Geneva 1996, p.5, quoted in S.K. Date-Bah, "Rights of Indigenous People in Relation to Natural Resources Development: an African's perspective" Vol. 16 No. 4 (1998), *Journal of Energy and Natural Resources Law*, 389 at 392.

> the dominant society, occupied a particular area before other population groups arrived. This is a description, which is valid in North and South America, and in some areas of the Pacific. In most of the world, however, there is very little distinction between the time at which tribal and other traditional people arrived in the region and the time at which other populations arrived. In Africa, for instance, there is no evidence to indicate that the Masai, the Pygmies or the San (Bushmen), namely peoples who have distinct social, economic and cultural features, arrived in the region they now inhabit long before other African populations. The same is true of some parts of Asia. The ILO therefore decided when it first began working intensively on these questions shortly after World War II, that it should refer to indigenous and tribal peoples. The intention was to cover a social situation, rather than to establish a priority based on whose ancestors had arrived in a particular area first. In addition, the description of certain population groups as tribal is more easily accepted by some governments than a description of those peoples as indigenous. The Convention makes no distinction in the way in which indigenous groups and tribal groups are treated. Both have the same rights under the ILO Convention No. 169.

Some minorities, particularly in the Niger Delta might feel they fall within the definition of tribal people. This could be a plausible interpretation, as the Convention does not distinguish 'minorities' from 'indigenous and tribal people'. However, the intent of the Convention was clearly not to distinguish minority ethnic groups living in a country with other homogenous groups, all of which can lay equal rights over their respective parts of national territory. Also, this approach is not advocated for at least the following reasons:

- It runs contrary to the spirit of the Convention, which was to protect the people who originally inhabited and were forcibly deprived of lands now dominated by others. These include the Aborigines of Australia, the Indians in the Americas, and the Maori of New Zealand.
- African states should ideally be concerned with nation building. Giving special rights to a particular group will not encourage this process.
- Existing constitutional rights and national laws for all citizens should provide adequate protection for all citizens. Where they are inadequate emphasis should be on amending and improving the law for all who suffer the situation in question, and not for special treatment to be given to a particular ethnic group.

This means that, in the interests of national unity, no particular tribe should be seen as having rights over natural resources under its land that are more than the rights of other tribes over the natural resources located under the territories within which they are residing. Thus, where ownership is vested in the state, this should apply to all resources in respect of all tribes. Where special rights over natural resources are granted, they should be available to every ethnic group under whose land such resources are located.

The protection of communities should be in the form of laws that give adequate protection to these ethnic groups; through the allocation of a greater percentage of proceeds from sale of the natural resource to the affected communities; and through ensuring that they are not left out of the development process. In line with this, the constitutional increase in the derivation allocation, from 3% to 13% is welcome. It is however a starting point, as the allocation based on derivation has undergone several erosions since independence, from 100% before the creation of states, to 3%.[11] This amount should go to the actual communities and not just to the state.

It is also necessary to mention the defunct Oil Mineral Producing Areas Development Commission (OMPADEC). This commission was set up by the Babangida administration "to address the difficulties and sufferings of inhabitants of the Niger Delta", but unfortunately failed to achieve its objectives. Throughout its period of existence, there were constant allegations of corruption and mismanagement, and little or no positive effects on the oil producing communities.

An Act establishing a Niger Delta Development Commission was recently passed by the National Assembly. The Niger Delta Development Commission Act of 1999 repealed the Oil Mineral Producing Areas Commission (OMPADEC) Decree 1999 and established the Niger Delta Development Commission. All oil producing states are to be member states of the NDDC. Those specifically mentioned as oil producing states are Abia, Akwa Ibom, Bayelsa, Cross River, Delta, Edo, Imo, Ondo and Rivers State. The Commission is to be under the Presidency and has the responsibility of overseeing and co-ordinating the sustainable development of the Niger Delta. The NDDC Act is yet to be implemented. One hopes that this effort to ameliorate the sufferings of the oil communities will be successful.

---

[11] See Ike Ogiune "Nigeria's Oil Revenues and the Oil Producing Areas" Vol. 17, No. 2 (1999) *JERL* 111: *The Price of Oil: Corporate Responsibility and Human Rights Violations in Nigeria's Oil Producing Communities,* Human Rights Watch 1999, at Chapter 4.

In summary oil communities can be adequately protected through municipal laws and regulations which take into account their special status and not through claims of indigenous ownership. The movements advocating community ownership of natural resources are aimed at redressing current imbalances. It is noteworthy that documents such as the Ogoni Bill of Rights and the Kaiama Declaration are not at all secessionist in character but are merely calls for justice and development by disadvantaged people.[12] It is possible that some might resist special treatment for all such communities. However, one is not advocating preferential treatment for any community, merely for adequate protection to be given to any community that suffers the peculiar deprivations of the communities of the Niger Delta. Oil might be commercially discovered in a totally different part of the country and the surrounding communities might now experience some of the environmental problems of the Niger Delta communities. When that happens, there will be new oil communities who will benefit from the enhanced treatment that the communities of the Niger Delta are agitating for.

Rights for injuries suffered as a result of oil industry activities

Individuals and communities that suffer environmental damage from oil industry activities have only a right of compensation. An injunction restraining the activities of an oil company is unlikely to be granted by any court because of the

[12] These documents are available at http://www.nigerianscholars.africanqueen.com. The Ogoni Bill of Rights is by the Ogoni people whilst the Karama Declaration was prepared by the Ijaws. Both are major Niger Delta ethnic groups.

strategic importance of the oil industry.[13] In this area the main law appears to be S.36 of Schedule 1 to the Petroleum Act 1969. This provision provides for the payment of "fair" and "adequate" compensation. Other provisions are Regs. 21 and 23 of the Petroleum Regulations, 1969 which speak of "fair" and "adequate" compensation respectively. These terms are highly subjective and are not defined within any enactment.

Sec. 36 Schedule 1 to the Act and Reg. 21 refer to unmentioned surface rights and to specified plants. However, so many rights and interests may be affected such as those pertaining to fish ponds, fish farms, water-ways, canals, wild life sanctuaries, etc. These and other rights should be specifically mentioned in these laws for there to be any effect. But even if that was the case, the imprecise and undefined phrases used make it difficult to ascertain what, if any, legal duty has been imposed on the operator. Again, even if clear legal duties existed, the individual would still be disadvantaged because of the absence of any provisions enforcing strict liability. For example, if Operator A did not 'exercise the rights conferred by his license or lease in such a manner as unreasonably to interfere with the exercise of any fishing rights' but nonetheless, an oil spill still occurred, the individual would be unprotected. This could easily happen. It is well known that oil spills can be attributed to several causes,[14] some of which may occur even under a 'reasonable' operator. When this happens the greater burden is borne by the party that can least afford it – the individual. A favourite

[13] See O. Adewale "Judicial Attitude to Environmental Hazards in the Nigerian Oil Industry", *The Petroleum Industry and the Nigerian Environment*, Proceedings of the 1985 Seminar, DPR, Environmental Planning and Protection Division, 44.

[14] Soga A. Awobajo, "An Analyses of Oil Spill Incidents; 1976 – 1980" *1981 Petroleum Industry and the Nigerian Environment* 57.

argument against the imposition of strict liability on the companies is that one cause for oil spills is sabotage, and such provisions would encourage this practice. Whilst sabotage is not to be encouraged, many people innocent of sabotage suffer unduly when there is no strict liability. It might be better to consider ways and means of discouraging sabotage and getting communities to have an interest in the protection of and the continuation of oil industry activities in their areas. Therefore there is the need for the communities to be given a financial stake of some sort in the industry.[15]

In some states there are edicts dealing with the procedure and quantum of compensation. An example is the Rivers State Minimum Crop Compensation Rates Edict 1973. In the process of arriving at a compensation figure, the parties invariably negotiate. It has been observed in an earlier study[16] that the ratio of the compensation demanded and that which is finally paid varies between 20:1 and 200:1. This disparity might be evidence of the superior might, knowledge and bargaining power of the oil company. It might also be because the communities are making exorbitant demands, which they know will be subject to stringent negotiation. Most claims are settled out of courts, not necessarily because the claimants are satisfied, but often because of poverty, ignorance and the expense and uncertainty of litigation.

---

[15] See a very clear exposition on this in Ike Oguine, "Nigeria's Oil Revenues and the Oil Producing Areas", Vol. 17, No. 2. *JERL* 111.

[16] Dine A. Gberesu, "What Constitutes Fair and Adequate Compensation in Nigerian Oil Industry", paper presented at the International Seminar on the Petroleum Industry and the Nigerian Environment, Nov. 9 – 12, 1987.

Litigation

The common law remedies of negligence, nuisance and the Rule in *Rylands* v. *Fletcher* are available for the person who elects to go to court.

Under negligence, the burden of proof is on the plaintiff, and this is especially difficult to discharge without specialised knowledge, which is usually not available to the average community plaintiff. In *J. Chinda and Ors* v *Shell BP Petroleum Company of Nigeria,*[17] the plaintiff sued the defendant company for the heat, noise and vibration resulting from the negligent management and control of the flare set used during gas flaring operations which had resulted in a lot of damage to the plaintiffs property. The judge held that the plaintiff could not prove any negligence on the part of the defendant in the management and control of the flare set. A similar conclusion was reached in *Anthony Atubin* v. *Shell BP Development Company of Nigeria* where the plaintiffs claimed that the defendant caused crude oil, gas and chemicals to escape from the pipelines under their control thereby destroying fishes in the lake and their farmland.[18]

For nuisance the main problems lie in the facts that damage must be proved that the plaintiff must have an interest in the land in question, and also that since public nuisance is a crime actionable by the state, an individual suing under this head must show that he has suffered damage over and above that suffered by the general public. In *Amos* v *Shell-BP*

---

[17] D. Currie *Pollution Cases and Materials* (West Publishers 1975) quoted in O.Adewale *supra*, note 13.

[18] Suit No. UCH/48/73 Ughelli High Court delivered on November 12, 1974

Petroleum Development Company of Nigeria and Another,[19] the plaintiffs in their representative capacity claimed general and special damages for injuries incurred as a result of the defendants' blocking of a creek in the course of their petroleum operations. As a result "farms were flooded and damaged, canoes could not bring goods to market or take produce to the outside world, and the whole commercial and agricultural life of the community absolutely stopped."[20]

The judge held that this action constituted public nuisance. However, without proof over and above that suffered by the general public the plaintiffs could not succeed in any claim for damages. Also an action for special damages in a representative capacity could not be maintained because any losses suffered were suffered separately and each individual must plead and prove his or her special individual loss. This is not easy to do for the average rural community.

It appears that a plaintiff's greatest chance of success lies in suing under the *Rule* in *Rylands* v *Fletcher*. From cases seen by this writer, more actions have been successful under this heading because petroleum operations are regarded as a non-natural use of land. While great sympathy is felt for the aggrieved individual, it is not felt here that petroleum operations in a major oil producing country like Nigeria should be termed a non-natural use of land.

Even when the plaintiff is successful the remedies applied by the court are likely to be insufficient. As earlier stated, it is virtually unthinkable for any court to issue an injunction restraining an oil company. Damages are therefore the most likely remedies which the court will give, and this is the often the only reason that the plaintiffs have gone to court in the

---

[19] Suit No. PHC/45/1972.

[20] Page 1. of the judgement.

first place. Unfortunately, the damages awarded in the past have often been paltry and not worth all the trouble.[21] The plaintiff may even find that the court awards the exact amount of compensation that was earlier offered by the defendant, as happened in the case of *Godspower Nweke* v. *Nigerian Agip Oil Company Ltd.*[22] When the plaintiffs appealed against the judgement, the Supreme Court was of the opinion that the claims should have been dismissed in its entirety because it was claimed by the defendants that the plaintiffs previously agreed to an amount offered by the defendant. Judicial attitude therefore appears to be weighted in favour of the oil companies.

The case of *F.B. Farah & Ors* v *The Shell Petroleum Development Company of Nigeria Ltd*, might lead one to conclude that the courts are becoming innovative. In this case, the defendants were held liable to pay compensation, solely under section 36 of the Petroleum Act.[23]

In summary, oil communities are inadequately protected by the law. This is a major reason for the various extra legal methods which they have adopted, including the taking of hostages and the forcible closures of oil installations. A notable example of the latter is the Nigerian LNG plant, which was scheduled to commence shipment on October 1, 1999. Protests of irate youths over demands for more development projects from the company, resulted in the plant being shut down for some days. It took the intervention of the highest levels of government before reopening and shipment on

---

[21] The Courts have even awarded an amount as low as N200.00 (approximately £15 sterling). See O. Adewale 1985 "Petroleum Industry and the Nigerian Environment" 44 at 46.

[22] (1976) 10 S.C. 101. See also O. Adewale (*Supra*) at pp. 49-50.

[23] For greater detail see F.O. Ayodele – Akaakar, "Legal Control of Petroleum Rehabilitation. The Poverty of Petroleum Law in Nigeria", Vol. 1, 1997, *The Nigeria Journal of Public Law*, 142.

October 8, 1999. Lasting solutions hinge around the enactment of adequate legislation, the creation of effective regulations and enhanced development within the oil communities.

Selected reading materials

O. Adewale "Judicial Attitude to Environmental Hazards in the Nigerian Oil Industry," *The Petroleum Industry and the Nigerian Environment*, Proceedings of the 1985 Seminar, (DPR, Environmental Planning and Protection Division) 44.

F. O. Ayodele–Akaakar "Legal Control of Pollution Rehabilitation: The Poverty of Petroleum Law in Nigeria," Vol. 1, 1997, *The Nigerian Journal of Public Law*, 214.

S.K. Date-Bah, "Rights of Indigenous People in Relation to Natural Resources Development: an African's Perspective, Vol. 16, No. 4, (1998) *JERL*, 389.

Ike Oguine "Nigeria's Oil Revenues and the Oil Producing Areas," Vol. 17, No.2 (1999) *JERL* 111.

Topic XIII

Topical issues in the petroleum industry

This chapter deals with selected topical issues that are relevant to the development of the Nigerian petroleum industry and Nigerian development.

These are:

- the acquisition of technology
- indigenous oil companies
- marginal fields
- The utilisation of revenues earned from petroleum.

The acquisition of technology

Most developing countries expect some technology transfer as a result of the oil industry activities within their territories. The extent of this transfer is dependent on government policy and the priority it places on the acquisition of technology.

Technology is defined to mean:[1]

> ...Systematic knowledge for the manufacture of a product, the application of a process or the rendering of a

---

[1] According to the Draft International Code of Conduct on the Transfer of Technology.

> service, whether that knowledge be reflected in an invention, an industrial design, a utility model, or a new plant variety, or in technical information or skills, or in the services and assistance provided by experts for the design, installation, operation or maintenance of an industrial plant or for the management of an industrial or commercial enterprise or its activities.

It should be noted that a technology transfer is first and foremost a transfer of knowledge and not just of a finished product that embodies high technology. A transfer occurs when a technology application that has been developed and applied by one organisation, is utilised and effectively applied by another organisation. For transfer to be possible, the personnel of the recipient organisation must be capable of applying the necessary knowledge required. Therefore, the people in question must have basic education at the very least. For this reason, the acquisition of technology in any state is linked with the level of education of the populace as illiterates or barely educated persons are not able to understand technical concepts. However, where people have the minimal knowledge, they can be trained.

In the area of technology acquisition there is a divergence of interest because transfer is not usually in the interests of the organisation that owns the technology. Huge amounts of time and resources will have been spent on the development of the technology in question and therefore the transferring organisation will naturally want to derive as many benefits as possible from its technology. On the other hand, the recipient state often wishes to freely acquire the technology, or to pay as little as possible.

In the municipal petroleum industry, transfer is usually governed by national legislation, and by contractual clauses.

In Nigeria the Petroleum Act 1969 provides in para. 38 of Schedule 1 that:

> The holder of an oil mining lease shall ensure that –
> a) within ten years from the grant of his lease –
> i) the number of citizens of Nigeria employed by him in connection with the lease in managerial, professional and supervisory grades (designated by him in a manner approved by the Minister) shall reach at least 75 per cent of the total number of persons employed by him in those grades, and
> ii) the number of citizens of Nigeria in any one such grade shall be not less than 60 per cent of the total and
> b) all skilled, semi-skilled and unskilled workers are citizens of Nigeria.

The Petroleum (Drilling and Production) Regulations provide for the recruitment and training of Nigerians and for scholarship schemes. The licensee or lessee is obliged to submit a detailed programme for recruitment/training and for scholarships, to the Minister for approval.

Clauses on technology acquisition in Nigerian exploration and production contracts centre on employment and training, and on title to equipment. The following samples are from Nigerian PSCs.

Sample 1

Employment and training of Nigerian personnel

- Each Year, the CONTRACTOR shall submit a detailed programme for recruitment and training for the following

Year in respect of its Nigerian personnel in accordance with the Petroleum Act 1969 and its amendments.

- Qualified Nigerians shall be employed in all non-specialised positions.
- Qualified Nigerians shall also be employed in specialised positions such as those in exploration, drilling, engineering, production, and finance. The CONTRACTOR shall have the right, subject to applicable laws, rules and regulations, to employ non-Nigerians in such specialised positions where qualified Nigerians are not available provided that the CONTRACTOR shall recruit and train Nigerians for such specialised positions such that the number of non-Nigerian staff shall be kept to a minimum.
- Competent professionals of the CORPORATION shall be attached to work with the CONTRACTOR from time to time and such officials and the CONTRACTOR's officials shall not be treated differently with regard to salaries and other benefits.
- Costs and expenses incurred in the recruitment and training of Nigerian personnel shall be included in Operating Costs.

Sample 2

Title to equipment

- CONTRACTOR shall finance the cost of purchasing all equipment to be used in Petroleum Operations in Nigeria pursuant to the Work Programmes and such equipment shall become the property of NNPC on arrival in Nigeria. The landed cost of such equipment purchased by

CONTRACTOR shall be included as Operating Costs and CONTRACTOR and NNPC shall have the right to use such equipment exclusively for Petroleum Operations in Nigeria during the effective period of this contract.

- CONTRACTOR'S right to use such purchased equipment shall cease with the termination or expiration (which ever is earlier) of this Contract.
- The provisions of paragraph (1) of this Article shall not apply to leased equipment belonging to foreign third parties, and such equipment may be freely exported from Nigeria in accordance with the terms of the applicable lease.
- All lands purchased or otherwise acquired by CONTRACTOR for the purposes of Petroleum Operations and all movable property utilised in the Contract Area and incorporated permanently in any premises, locations and structures for the purposes of Petroleums hereunder shall become property of NNPC. Upon termination of this contract, pursuant to Article 21 CONTRACTOR shall transfer same to NNPC.
- Subject to Article 11 (iii) hereof, all fixed assets purchased or otherwise acquired by CONTRACTOR for the purposes of Petroleum Operations hereunder shall become the property of NNPC. Upon termination of this Contract pursuant to Article 21, CONTRACTOR shall transfer such fixed assets to NNPC.
- All fixed assets, which have been acquired for temporary use by CONTRACTOR in Petroleum Operations hereunder, shall be the property of CONTRACTOR and NNPC shall not be obligated to reimburse CONTRACTOR for the cost thereof. NNPC shall reimburse CONTRACTOR, as part of the cost of

exploration costs, reasonable amounts for use or rental of the fixed assets that are the property of CONTRACTOR. Such reimbursement shall be in accordance with the usage or rental charges current in the international petroleum industry.

- NNPC shall have the right of first refusal to purchase from CONTRACTOR all materials, machinery or equipment other than fixed assets that are the property of NNPC, purchased or otherwise acquired by CONTRACTOR for the purpose of Petroleum Operations hereunder. CONTRACTOR shall give to NNPC a notice in writing of CONTRACTOR'S desire to dispose of such material, machinery or equipment. Such notice shall be accompanied by an inventory of the materials, equipment and machinery that are the property of CONTRACTOR. NNPC may exercise its option to purchase the same by notice in writing to CONTRACTOR within (60) sixty days, from the date of CONTRACTOR'S notice. NNPC and the CONTRACTOR shall negotiate the purchase price of the materials, equipment and machinery specified in the CONTRACTOR'S notice.

Nigerian clauses are not regarded as particularly stringent as examples of contracts imposing greater training obligations are to be found in other countries. Nevertheless, there is a high degree of indigenisation in the oil producing companies, as a result of the strict enforcement of training and employment clauses in the 1970s.

Clauses giving title to equipment to the state are more symbolic than effective. First of all, constant research and development render the newest technologies obsolete after the first few years, and most certainly, after the normal duration of an oil-mining lease. Secondly, such clauses encourage the operator companies to lease anything that can be leased, particularly those that are of real value. Thirdly, since equipment used in petroleum operations becomes the property of NNPC, it (NNPC) also has sole responsibility for the removal of any installations, whenever petroleum operations cease. For offshore abandonment, these costs can be quite substantial, and in such instances, this type of clause is quite detrimental to the interests of the nation.

Indigenous oil companies

An indigenous oil company is one in which at least 60% of the shares are owned by Nigerians. This has been the accepted definition since 1991, when the indigenous producers were encouraged through positive policies put in place by the then Federal Minister for Petroleum Resources.

The Draft bill to regulate the development of marginal fileds[2] which is the brainchild of the Association of Indigenous Petroleum Explorers and Producers (NAIPEC) defines an indigenous producer in line with this definition, as one where 60% or more shares are beneficially owned directly or indirectly by Nigerian citizens and/or associations of Nigerian citizens.

In the real sense the term 'indigenous oil company' includes both privately and publicly owned companies, and therefore, any oil company owned by the government falls

---

[2] This draft is currently being considered by the National Assembly. It is in the Federal Republic of Nigeria official Gazette No. 44, Vol. 87 of 16th June, 2000, SI No. SB 41. A Bill for an Act to make provisions regulating the development of marginal fields and to encourage holders of marginal fields to farm out any marginal fields held by them to indigenous oil companies.

within this definition. This would include the Nigerian National Petroleum Corporation (NNPC) and subsidiaries such as the Nigerian Petroleum Development Corporation (NPDC). In fact, they are indigenous oil companies. They share a lot of common problems and the reasons why they should be nurtured are generally the same for the private and public companies. However, there are a few differences when the state is in the market place, not the least being the presence of sovereign might behind the government entity.

In previous decades viable indigenous oil industries in developing countries were state owned and consultants and specialists who believed strongly in the growth and development of Third World countries, strongly advocated for an increased role in exploration and production for national oil companies.[3]

Such viewpoints have helped the rise of the indigenous companies from developing countries, both state and privately owned. Now indigenous companies include all the national oil companies, amongst which is the Saudi Arabian Aramco. This company controls the national oil industry in Saudi Arabia and – by virtue of that fact alone – ranks as the world's largest company in terms of reserves and production.

Whilst the term 'indigenous companies' incorporates both public and privately owned companies, this section focuses on the private oil companies in Nigeria for two reasons. The first

---

[3] A very good example is Michael Tanzer who showed, in his writings, that the following assumptions were myths:

(1) That only the big oil companies vital exploration technology
(2) That only the big oil companies have the capital necessary for exploration and development, and
(3) That only the big oil companies can afford the risk of oil exploration. Michael Tanzer "Oil Exploration Strategies: Alternatives for the Third World" in Petter Nore and Terisa Turner, *Oil and Class Struggle*, Zed Press 1980, 89, at 91-92.

is that these companies need special attention because they do not have the backing of sovereign might that the national oil companies have. Secondly this term is seen in Nigeria as referring only to the private indigenous entity. So one finds that even the Nigerian Production and Development Company (NPDC) is not a member of the private organisation established for the benefit of indigenous producers, the Nigerian Association of Indigenous Production and Exploration Companies (NAIPEC). However, the listing of indigenous companies by the Department of Petroleum Resources includes both genres. Whatever aids the growth of the private indigenous producers also benefits any state entities. A strong and viable oil industry in Nigeria is surely one where both types of companies are playing vital roles.

Legal definitions apart, the private indigenous producer can be classified as an independent from a developing country. Viewed in that light, and with knowledge of the meteoric use of some American independents, one appreciates that these companies, given the right stimuli and environment, have the capacity to grow far beyond the expectations of even the positive onlooker. The term 'independent' was first used by Rockefeller to mean a non-Standard Oil company. These included Texaco, Gulf and Phillips which themselves grew stupendously large and integrated. Therefore the definition of the term changed to mean any company that was not integrated. Again many companies have grown out of this definition and are now generally classified as majors e.g. Amoco, ARCO, Tenneco, and Occidental to name a few. The merger of BP, Amoco and Arco in recent times has led to the emergence of the world's second largest oil company. The moral of this seems to be that any small oil company has the capacity to grow stupendously, given the right environment, management, and of course, providence.

In Nigeria, there would be hardly any indigenous producers today were it not for the policy shift in 1991 which resulted in several awards being made to Nigerian companies. This policy was aimed at:

- expanding the scope of Nigerian participation in the oil industry and diversifying the sources of investment and funds inflow; and
- increasing exploration efforts in Nigeria and thereby increasing the oil and gas reserves base.

This application of this policy was sufficient to give birth to the indigenous companies.

As at May 1999, at least 54 indigenous oil companies had existing licences. Sixteen of these – mainly the newest allocations awarded by the Abubakar regime – were revoked by the democratic government. Several others had their licenses revoked because of inactivity.

Criticisms of indigenous companies

Major criticisms of indigenous oil companies stem from (1) the way and manner in which the awards are made (2) the type of companies that have been given acreages, (3) the types of acreages that have been given to these companies.

The award of licences to indigenous contractors appears to have been largely influenced by the extent to which prominent shareholders have been connected to the government. In the past, competence and expertise have not necessarily been paramount. With respect to the first spate of licences, the government intentionally gave licences out to several already successful businessmen. According to the Petroleum Minister who awarded these initial concessions this was deliberate, and from his words quoted below, some of these businessmen were in fact persuaded to take the acreages.

> One area of oil development one is really proud to mention is the one of indigenous participation in Oil Exploration and Production. Three things led me to it. The first one was that I did not see a single indigenous company producing virtually anything at all (sic). Those that did bought them over from foreign companies. Secondly, I discovered that none of the joint venture operators owned any drilling rig. They rented them all from oil service engineering companies. Finally I also discovered that a lot of the chairmen of the big international oil companies were not engineers or scientists at all. Some prominent ones were Accountants and Businessmen. The idea of indigenous participation required a lot of persuasion to the businessmen who found it daunting. It was only later on, when a bonanza air was given to the idea that the flood of requests started. I am very delighted that most of the successful ones are those with whom we started from the beginning. But, we were determined to prove the point, namely, that our people can do it.[4]

Nearly a decade later, some of the earlier companies are thriving. Consolidated Oil and Summit Oil had made the first discoveries by 1993. Both of these companies were owned by

---

[4] Jubril Aminu "Resurrecting our Buried hopes and Opportunities" in Siddi E. Mkpandiok, *Energy Crisis in Nigeria: Causes, Effects, Solutions* Pengassan 1999, 177.

successful businessmen.[5] However, of the several companies awarded prior to 1999, the majority have been described as passive or inactive. Some have made no progress and ideally, should have mandatorily relinquished their blocks at the stipulated times and in accordance with Nigerian statutory law. The licenses of most of these companies were revoked a few months ago as stated above.

On the whole, cannot say that persons successful in other business will be just as successful in the oil business. The few persons conversant with the oil industry who were awarded allocations are still in operation: Many of the inactive companies belong to businessmen or those with powerful connections who could not cope with or were not prepared for the high amounts and long investment periods of the industry.

To date, the allocations have remained highly dependent on the connections of the promoters than on anything else. This is particularly evident if one considers the recently revoked deep offshore acreages,[6] where only one of the older indigenous companies got a licence and not one multinational was successful. Of the new entrants at the time, quite a few were connected with past and present government functionaries, all of whom had no practical oil industry experience.

A few months later, licenses of the few non-functioning indigenous companies at the time were revoked. In March 2000, the government commenced a new licensing round, offering up deep and ultra-deep blocks to prospective companies.[7] The Guidelines for the License Round are however very stringent and the conditions do not favour

---

[5] Summit Oil was owned by the late Chief MKO Abiola and failed to maintain its initial lead largely for political reasons.

[6] Revoked during the first few days of the Obasanjo administration which was sworn in on 29 May , 1999.

[7] See http://www.nigeria-licenseround.com

indigenous companies. It appears that there has been a policy shift that is not in their favour.

Some feel that deep offshore acreages are really best given to those with some expertise because of the level of technology and expertise required. In fact during the 1991 bidding rounds these blocks were reserved for the more experienced companies. A little later, 4 indigenous companies were given blocks. These were Allied Energy and Natural Resources, Famfa Oil, Noreast Petroleum and Yinka Folawiyo. Famfa and Noreast have made discoveries and Famfa's find is a major discovery. The deep offshore is said to contain large wells. This is probably why majors and new indigenous companies alike more eagerly seek these acreages, as opposed to the more modest reserves of the marginal fields. Even with deep offshore acreages, technology transfer and real benefits to the nation are still possible if allocations are made to the committed entrepreneur. For the average businessman it is more tempting to take the upfront payments, and other attractive amounts (if a discovery is made), reinvest the money, or simply relax and enjoy a comfortable life style. Any polices or strategies for growth are better geared towards the entrepreneur with a vision rather than for the businessman who is only after profits.

Marginal fields

A marginal field is a non-producing field whose economics is not considered robust enough using conventional development methods under the prevailing fiscal regime.[8] There are several

[8] See Petroleum News July 1999, quoted in Y. Omorogbe "*Fundamental Issues relating to the Development of Marginal Fields in Nigeria*" Vol. 3, No. 4 (1999) *Modern Practice Journal of Finance and Investment Law.*

such fields in the country, mainly in the Niger Delta. Marginal fields are governed by the Petroleum (Amendment) Decree No. 23 of 1996, which provides for the insertion of a new paragraph 16A after paragraph 16 of Schedule 1 to the Petroleum Act 1969. This law defines a marginal field as "such field as the Head of State, Commander-in-Chief of the Armed Forces may from time to time, identify as a marginal field." The law allows the holder of an OML, with the consent of the Head of State, to farm out any marginal field within his area. It also allows the Head of State to farm out a marginal field which has been left unattended for at least ten years. The Head of State 'shall not give his consent' to a farm-out unless he is satisfied that it is in the public interest to do so, that the field has been unattended for ten years, and that the parties to the farm-out are acceptable to the government.

Arguments against production from marginal fields centre around the fact that it is uneconomic. For a country such as Nigeria that operates under an OPEC quota – it means the substitution of high cost oil for low cost, uneconomically produced oil. This is in fact a paramount point, and would definitely rank predominantly if it was not for the fact that the marginal fields are expected to be farmed out to small indigenous operators.

Since such companies are the proposed beneficiaries of the farm-out, the viewpoint here is that the question of its feasibility or practicability cannot be decided solely from an economic perspective. National development and technology transfer perspectives are equally important. For any country there are major differences when a critical service is being performed by nationals, as opposed to a foreign company. Not only is the gross national product (GNP) positively affected but positive flows of increased ancillary revenues, technology acquisition and development, and other positive externalities also accrue. Some fear that the Nigerian companies will in fact, not be actually involved in the production and development of their fields, and most or none of the expected benefits will materialise because most of them will simply assign or transfer their interests to foreign operators. It must be said that this fear may not be misplaced; it is, in fact, much easier to take this alternative. In the past, some of these companies were not as interested in exploration and production, as in the crude oil that they were invariably allocated by the government, to cushion them against the huge amounts which they were supposedly expending. However, if the will is there, it is possible to enact legislation which expressly prohibits the indigenous companies from assigning their marginal field to foreign operators, while at the same time allowing for partnerships and technical assistance. A supervisory body, such as the Department of Petroleum Resources, could be charged with the responsibility of ensuring that the provisions of such legislation are adhered to. Therefore this potential outcome can be curtailed, if the will exists.

On the whole, the merits of marginal field production far outweigh the demerits, if the beneficiaries are indigenous companies. If they are not, then most of the benefits no longer apply, and the bad economy of developing a marginal field at the expense of a profitable one then becomes paramount.

State policy and the indigenous marginal field producer

The indigenous producer is heavily dependent on the state for survival and growth, as the policy of a state plays a decisive role in the success of its home companies and in the development of various strategic industries.

It is not always remembered that the international oil industry has been decisively shaped and influenced by the policies and actions of the home governments of the major companies. As an example, the American governments dissolution of the Standard Oil empire in 1911, totally changed the face of the industry and allowed for the massive growth of companies outside the Standard 'Family' many of which are among of the worlds largest companies today.[9] Throughout the history of the industry, the major companies have always positively benefited from the actions of their home governments. Any studies of the rise and growth of the big companies or of the diplomatic interventions of the home governments bear eloquent testimonies as to the importance of positive interventions from companies' home countries.

Much smaller companies such as Nigerian indigenous oil producers are far more vulnerable to home state policies and actions. Such companies are often extremely dependent on policies that favourably encourage their growth. Often the capital that they need can only be obtained internationally and then only with some sort of positive action by the company's home government.[10] So far it appears that very few developing country governments have active incentives to encourage indigenous oil producers. In Nigeria these companies are not

---

[9] For more details see Y. Omorogbe 'Indigenous Companies and the Nigerian Petroleum Industry in A.O. Obilade (ed.), *A Blueprint for Nigerian Law*, Faculty of Law, University of Lagos 1995, especially 118 – 122.

[10] A Nigerian oil entrepreneur states his experience in sourcing for funds from an American bank which required a guarantee from the Nigerian government that they would allow profits made to be repatriated to repay the loan. This could not be obtained and the loan was not granted – for fuller detail see Y. Omorogbe *op. cit.*

even covered by any legislation and therefore, they operate at a disadvantage.[11]

Any state policy in favour of indigenous companies is likely to be expensive for the state at the initial stages. However, if these companies are successful, the rewards for the country as a whole are enormous. Then, a strong indigenous oil industry will truly emerge. It is not always realised that a strong national oil company and several major foreign companies do not really add up to a strong indigenous industry in the same way as would be the case if there were also a few viable private indigenous companies. Given the right policies and the right environment such companies can function as unofficial vehicles of state oil policy even better than an NOC because they do not have to be bogged down by uneconomic and/or political considerations. Secondly, as discussed earlier, there will be a much greater spill over effect in the nation as a result of the fact that these companies are owned by nationals.

The utilisation of revenues earned from petroleum

Nigerian governments have, in the past, set up schemes to utilise revenues from the oil industry to achieve certain objectives. These schemes are the Petroleum Trust Fund (PTF) and the Oil Mineral Producing Areas Development Commission (OMPADEC). At the time of writing the

---

[11] One country that does is Korea.. Gordon Barrows 'A Survey of incentives in recent petroleum contracts' in Nicky Beredjick – Thomas *Walde Petroleum Investment Policies in Developing Countries*, Graham and Trotman, London, 1988 p.225 at 241

National Assembly passed a bill for the establishment of the Niger Delta Development Commission.[12]

The Petroleum (Special) Trust Fund

Presently the fate of the Petroleum (Special) Trust Fund (PTF) is uncertain. The Obasanjo administration dissolved the Board soon after assumed government and appointed an Interim Management Committee which was mandated to manage existing commitments and to take an inventory of the PTF.

The Petroleum Trust Fund (PTF) was established by the Petroleum (Special) Trust Fund Decree No. 25 of 1994. According to section 1(1) the money in this account consists of all the monies received from the sale price of petroleum products less the marketers' margin. The Fund was under the control of the Head of State,[13] and was managed by the Petroleum (Special) Trust Fund Management Board. The Board had very wide powers of control and approval. It was authorised to deal with projects in any of the following sectors:[14]

- road and road transportation;
- railway transportation and waterways;
- education;
- health;
- food supply;
- water supply;

---

[12] Both these commissions are discussed under Topic XII below.

[13] Act 1(3). In addition to this Act 13(1) also provides for other sums of money to be paid into the Funds, such as subventions from the Federal Government, and subventions, fees and charges for services rendered or publications made by the Fund.

[14] Act 3(1)(d).

- security services;
- alternative sources of energy;
- rural development programmes; and
- such other sectors as may be approved from time to time.

The Fund had well over 100 billion naira, which was spent in several areas such as road repairs, the rehabilitation of teaching hospitals and universities, water supply projects, the purchase of drugs and of educational materials.[15]

It is noteworthy that the tenure of the Fund coincided with Nigeria's lowest depths of development. This is not to imply that the Fund recorded no achievements but to emphasize that since Nigeria's major problem was bad management more than insufficient money, the creation of a Trust Fund could not make any appreciable difference to the development of the state.

Selected reading materials

Alegimenlen O., "Issues in the Acquisition of Petroleum Development Technology for Third World States," *OPEC Review* (Summer 1991) 123.

Alegimenlen O., "Acquisition of Petroleum Development Technology: a Synopsis of the Nigerian Experience."

Omorogbe Y., "Indigenous Companies and the Nigerian Petroleum Industry," in A. O. Obilade (ed.) *A Blueprint for Nigerian Law*, Faculty of Law, University of Lagos 1995

[15] See Y. Omorogbe "Petroleum Subsidies and the Petroleum Trust Fund. The Nigerian Alternative" Vol.15, Issue 6 *OGLTR* 203, for some analysis of the PTF.

Omorogbe Y., "Fundamental Issues relating to the Development of Marginal Fields in Nigeria" Vol. 3 No.... *Modern Practice Journal of Finance and Investment Law*

Omorogbe Y., "Petroleum Subsidies and the Petroleum Trust Fund: the Nigerian Alternative," Vol. 15 Issue 6, 1997 *OGLTR* 203.

Topic XIV

Nationalisation and privatisation

Whilst the 1970s can be described as the era of nationalisation, the 1990s will be better remembered for privatisation.

Nationalisation

Nationalisation is the legal taking of the property of an alien. In earlier times, it was more commonly referred to as expropriation.

Nationalisation is lawful under international law. However, there is divergence of opinion concerning the conditions for lawful taking of property, and the amount of compensation payable. Traditional international law states that expropriation is lawful if the following conditions are met.

(1) if it is not discriminatory
(2) if it is for a public purpose, and
(3) if prompt, adequate and effective compensation is paid

These traditional international law rules are also collectively called the Cordell Hull Formula, after the United

States Secretary of State Cordell Hull who had cause to restate these principles in 1938.

'Prompt' refers to the time of payment. It is expected that compensation should be paid in time, that is, soon after the property has been taken. This is a necessarily subjective condition as no period of time is stipulated.

'Adequate' refers to the amount of compensation payable. Again this is a subjective term. Is a compensation payment adequate if it represents the net book value of the investment or the market value? Should the future profits and goodwill also be calculated in arriving at an adequate amount? These are unresolved issues and a look at state practice reveals wide divergences.

'Effective' compensation refers to compensation which is in a readily convertible currency. Normal compensation in kind will not be regarded as effective.

These legal rules came into force before the independence/emergence of states outside the Western Hemisphere and thus are regarded by many states as not being representative of what they regard as the law in this area. For these states, expropriation should be governed more by the municipal law of the host state than by international law. The position of these states is contained in the United Nations General Assembly Resolution on Permanent Sovereignty over National Resources[1] which states that:

> Nationalisation, expropriation or requisitioning shall be based on grounds or reasons of public utility, security or the national interest which are recognised as over riding purely individual or private interests, both domestic and foreign. In such cases the owner shall be paid appropriate

[1] Res. 1803 (XVII) of 1962

> compensation in accordance with the rules in force in the state taking such measures in the exercise of its sovereignty and in accordance with international law. In any case when the question of compensation gives rise to a controversy, the national jurisdiction of the state taking such measures shall be exhausted. However, upon agreement by sovereign states and other parties concerned, settlement of the dispute should be made though arbitration or international adjudication...

Later, the United Nations Charter of Economic Rights and Duties of States[2] declared that every state has the right;

> to nationalise, expropriate or transfer ownership of foreign property in which case appropriate compensation should be paid, taking into account its relevant laws and regulations and all circumstances that the state considers pertinent. In any case where the question of compensation gives rise to a controversy, it shall be settled by the domestic law of the nationalising state and by its tribunals, unless it is freely and mutually agreed by all states concerned that other peaceful means be sought on the basis of the sovereign equality of states and in accordance with the principle of free choice of means.

These two resolutions differ in that the former states that dispute settlement shall be internationalised, whilst the latter refers to resolution under municipal law. They both agree that 'appropriate' compensation is what is payable, and not 'prompt, adequate and effective' compensation. A study of treaties and writings of distinguished international lawyers lends weight to the opinion that 'appropriate' compensate is

---

[2] United Nations General Assembly Resolution 3281 (XXIX) of 1974.

more representative of the current position. One finds that even countries such as the United States, which clearly states its belief in the continuing validity of the Cordell Hull Formula, nonetheless has entered into several bilateral treaties with various states, upholding the classical standard. One has to ask why it is necessary to enter into bilateral treaties to uphold a rule of international law. The only reason why such a treaty could be necessary appears to be because the rule in question has been or is in the process of being eroded.

On the whole, the weight of evidence favours the emergence of a new standard of appropriate compensation for the nationalisation of alien property.

The oil nationalisations

There have been a few nationalisations concerning the oil industry. The following are the major arbitrations concerned with oil industry nationalisations.

1. *Texaco* v *Libya* (1978) 17 ILM 1,
2. *Aminoil Case* (*Kuwait* v *American Independent Oil Company*) (1982) 21 ILM 976
3. *BP Case* (*U.K* v *Libya*) (1974) 53 ILR 297
4. *Liamco Case* (*Libyan American Oil Co.* v *Libya*) (1981) 20 ILM 1
5. *Amoco Case* (*U.S.* v *Iran*) (1988) 27 ILM 1314.

These cases have contributed towards the enunciation of international law principles on or relating to compensation.

Presently, the international climate is veering away from nationalisation. First of all, the poorer states desire foreign investment, and nationalisation scares away investment capital. Secondly, there is a tendency towards privatisation, as the state has tended to be less than efficient in business and in the administration of public utilities.

Privatisation

Broadly speaking the process of privatisation deals with the whole or partial removal of a public undertaking from the control or ownership of the State. In practice there are differing extents to which this divestiture can take.

At the lowest level, there is the process of commercialisation or corporatisation. This is the commercial orientation of a state owned enterprise (SOE) and may often not include any removal of state ownership at all. It is expected that the process of commercialisation/corporatisation should lead to the conversion of an SOE into a limited liability company even if it remains 100% state-owned. However, in Nigeria this has not necessarily been the case. Some do not consider commercialisation to be genuine privatisation but others see it as a necessary step towards 'true' privatisation.

At the other extreme there is denationalisation. As its name implies it is the opposite of total state ownership (nationalisation) and leads, to the total divestiture of the state. Many privatisations are not this extreme in the sense that the state retains percentages of the company in question. Several privatisations involve the State retaining a shareholding that might even be as much as 50 percent.

Some might feel that the retention of a substantial percentage by the state negates the divestiture process as it still retains a critical controlling interest. It is however important to realise that in privatisation 'the State may be in retreat, but it has not left the market place altogether.[3] The fact is that the state continues to act as a regulator, through its laws, through the shareholding that it retainer or through both.

The method of regulation though shareholding is used by all nations, not just those in the developing world. The following quote is instructive.

> A system of golden shares has been used been used in privatisation operations in France, U.K and most recently, Belgium. Though a special share the government retains special rights which may include special voting and/or blocking rights. More specifically, they may be designed to prevent foreign take-overs. Although the EC Treaty does not include any instruments for privatisation, the influence by the Community (i.e. the EC Commission) has been more indirect, for example, by way of assessing the extent to which these golden shares are discriminatory and as such contrary to EU law. A recent example of golden shares is the share retained by the Belgian government in the company Distrigaz after the sales of the remaining 50 percent shares held by the State. This golden share allows the government to veto decisions, which could affect national energy policy. The prerogative of the State (the golden share) is linked to the defence of the public interest *inter alia* the security of supply.[4]

Even where denationalisation occurs the state still plays a regulatory role by virtue of the sovereignty that it exercises

---

[3] Catherine J. Redgwell "Privatisation and Environmental Regulation: Some General Observations," Vol. 15, No. 1, Feb., 1997 *JERL* 33 at 36.

[4] Martha M. Roggenkamp "Implications of Privatisation, Liberalisation and Integration of Networkhound Energy Systems," Vol. 15, No. 1, Feb., 1991 *JERL* 51 at 53.

over its territory.

The aim of a state which desires a successful privatisation programme is to ensure the existence of a regulatory regime which is straight forward, free of bottlenecks, and which encourages investments whilst protecting the interests of the state in question.

Reasons for privatisation

Government privatise for different reasons. The following are among the major reasons.

(1) Budgetary relief from the financial and administrative burdens of certain state enterprises.

(2) The need for a particular sector of the economy to achieve increased efficiency.

(3) The implementation of certain policy objectives. For example, some privatisations in countries such as Bangladesh, Canada, Chile and the Philippines involved failing private companies which the government acquired with the intention of returning them to the private sector at the earliest possible opportunity.[5]

(4) The need to earn more revenue.

(5) The desire for a wide distribution of ownership of the industry in question, possibly so as to establish a strong middle class and/or to achieve effective worker participation.

(6) To promote efficiency in the chosen sector through demonopolisation and the fostering of competition

---

[5] Charles Vuylsteke, Vol. I, *Techniques of Privatisation of State - Owned Enterprises*. World Bank Technical Paper Number 88, 1988 1 BRD, 57 at note 47.

Methods of privatisation

Some common ways through which privatisation is achieved are:

(1) The public offering of shares
(2) Private sales of shares
(3) Sales of assets
(4) New private investments in the state enterprise in question
(5) Lease and management contracts.

Public offering of shares

The state may decide to sell to the public a designated percentage (or all) of its holdings in the enterprise in question. The main advantage of this is that wide - spread shareholding can be achieved, provided specific mechanisms are utilised. These include restricting the percentage of foreign ownership and the total number of shares that may be owned by one legal entity.

Public offerings are handled as primary issues even through, technically speaking; it is a secondary distribution of government - held shares.

Private sales of shares

Under this method the state privately sells the shares in question to a single purchaser or group of purchasers. The procedure could be through the full competitive process or through direct negotiations with procedures for identifying potential users.

Private sales can suffer from a lack if transparency, as

compared with public offerings. However, detailed guidelines can minimise this problem. This method is preferred for weak enterprises or those, which require strong owners with requisite expertise for the state. An advantage is that the prospective owner or owners can be evaluated and the selection based on ability to bring in the required benefits.

Sales of assets

Privatisation can also occur when the state sells off assets, as opposed to shares in a venture. Assets can only be sold privately unless the government includes the assets as part of a corporate entity that is to be privatised by public offering. It is also possible for the government to contribute assets as part of its obligations to a new company formed with the private sector. The shares received by the government can then be sold.

New private placements

This form of privatisation does not entail any divestiture by the state. Instead the equity in the company is increased and the balance sold to private entities. This is mainly achieved through an increase in share capital which has the effect of diluting the percentage held by the government.

Lease and management contracts

Under lease and management contracts the state retains the assets of the industry in question but leases them out to be managed by the private entity. Often lease and management contracts lead to a privatisation of the infrastructure. However, it is also normal for the government to continue the arrangement for a long period of time. In such a case the privatisation is in fact limited to management and operations.

All these methods have been utilised in the course of the privatisation exercise in Nigeria.

Privatisation in Nigeria

Privatisation in Nigeria became a stated policy of the Nigerian government in 1988 when it embarked on the Privatisation and Commercialisation programmes. The goals of these programmes were:

(1) To improve the efficiency of the various government owned enterprises through a redefining of the roles of the supervising ministry and the public enterprises.

(2) To reduce the financial commitment of the Government towards the enterprises slated for privatisation.

(3) To increase participation of Nigerian citizens in the industries in question.

In pursuance of these objectives, the government promulgated the Privatisation and Commercialisation Decree which designated 111 enterprises for full or partial privatisation, 35 for full or partial commercialisation, and 117 smaller companies owned by the various river basin development authorities, for outright sale.

By 1993 when the body charged with the responsibility of privatisation/commercialisation - the Technical Committee on Privatisation and Commercialisation – submitted its report to the Government 86 public enterprises out of the 111 mentioned above had been privatised as follows:[6]

Sector	Number	Privatisation
Development	1	Full
Oil Marketing Corporation	3	Partial
Cement Plant	3	Partial
Hotels and Tourism	2	Full
Textiles	3	Full
Transport Companies	1	Full
Salt Companies	2	Full
Food and Beverages	6	Full
Insurance Companies	14	Full
Flour Mills	1	Full
Dairy Companies	2	Full
Construction and Engineering	4	Full
Commercial and Merchant Banks	10	Full
Agricultural & Livestock Production	18	Full
Others	14	Full
Total	**86**	

All the non-water assets were successfully disposed of.

Whilst the industrial concerns were many in number, no major industries were involved. Large industries such as the paper and steel mills; sugar companies and vehicle assembly plants remained untouched. Also the utility monopolies such as the National Electric Power Authority and Nigerian Telecommunications Limited and the Nigerian National Petroleum Corporation were on the commercialisation list and not the privatisation list.

During the Abacha regime, while privatisation was

[6] Hamzat Zayyad, "A Case Study of Nigeria's Privatisation" *This Day* Saturday, September 26, 1998, pp. 19 and 37.

invariably mentioned in each yearly budget, little was done to encourage it. However the Abubakar administration showed more commitment and enacted a new law titled Public Enterprises (Privatisation and Commercialisation) Decree 1999. This law was enacted on May 10, 1999 and backdated to December 1998. It is the second law directly dealing with privatisation. Under this law NNPC is also slated for full commercialisation.[7] However the latter law lists several NNPC subsidiaries for partial privatisation. These are:

(1) Port Harcourt Refinery
(2) Kaduna Refinery and Petrochemicals
(3) Warri Refinery and Petrochemicals
(4) Eleme Petrochemicals Company Ltd
(5) Pipelines Product and Marketing Company Limited
(6) Nigerian Petroleum Development Company Limited
(7) Nigeria Gas Company Limited.

In the downstream sector, the following three marketing companies are to be fully privatised.

(1) Unipetrol Plc
(2) National Oil and Chemical Company Ltd
(3) African Petroleum Plc

According to the Decree, partial privatisation involves the government retaining a maximum 40% shares in the company in question, and with 'strategic investor participation' being a maximum of 40%. The balance of 20% is to be held by Nigerian individuals. It should be noted that the Nigerian individual percentage could be more if, for example, either the Government or the strategic investor does not take up its

[7] Privatisation and Commercialisation Act 1988; 2nd Schedule Part II, Public Enterprises (Privatisation and Commercialisation) Decree 1999.

maximum allocated percentage. Section 5 regulates the sale of shares to Nigerians and provides that:

(1) the shares shall be sold 'on the basis of equality of States...'This means in effect, that a quota system will apply to ensure that no particular ethnic group is favoured during the privatisation exercise.
(2) 1% shall be reserved for the staff of the enterprise in question 'and the shares shall be held in trust by the public enterprises for its employees'. What precisely this means will be clearer as the privatisation exercise proceeds.
(3) No individual subscriber may hold more than 0.1% of the equity shares of any privatised public enterprise. This sub-section is to attempt to ensure an even distribution of shares, and to stop one or few individuals from buying all the available shares.

A comparison of nationalisation and privatisation

Nationalisation and privatisation are progammes entered into for the purpose of actualising state objectives at particular times.

Nationalisation is good for the national identity and for ensuring control over one's resources. The problem is that the state is often bad at administering and running businesses efficiently and/or profitably. Privatisation thus becomes the more pragmatic option and the favoured alternative at this time.

Selected reading materials

Privatisation

There are several works on privatisation in general, but little or nothing on the ongoing Nigerian privatisation. The student is encouraged to regularly read *The Guardian* and *This Day*, both of which regularly and efficiently report on investment and energy issues. World Bank and IMF publications are also generally informative and give case studies of actual privatisations e.g. *Privatisation: Principles and Practice*, The World Bank and IFC 1995

Nationalisation

There are numerous very good works in this area and these few works are but a sampling.

1. Any good textbook on international law e.g.
   a. Brownlie, I., *Principles of Public International Law*
   b. J. Dugard, *International Law: A South African Perspective*, A. Juta and Co, 1994.
2. J.E.S. Fawcett – Audrey Parry, *Law and International Resources Conflicts*.
3. S.K.B. Asante 'International Law and Foreign Investment: A Reappraisal' (1988) 37 *ICLQ* 588

Topic XV

Dispute settlement

Types of dispute settlement

It is inevitable that disputes must arise. The question is how to resolve such disputes in a manner acceptable to the parties concerned. The methods of dispute settlement are the same regardless of the type of industry and therefore any good book in this area will be of great relevance.

Renegotiation of the terms regulating the subject matter of the dispute is usually the first step, particularly when the parties are concerned with maintaining their long-term relationship. Negotiation involves just the parties and their chosen representatives and the aim is to work out a solution acceptable to the parties.

Such renegotiation can be provided for under the contract. Renegotiation clauses are one of the best means of resolving disputes, as negotiation is one of the less acrimonious alternatives for dispute resolution. Renegotiaton clauses provide for a review of terms, either at periodic intervals or if stated events occur. Preferably such clauses should be precise, and drafted according to the wishes of the parties. In practical terms, hardship, *force majeure*, and 'most favoured company' clauses can function as renegotiation clauses if their terms so specify.

If negotiation fails then resolution is likely to be by one of the following options:

- The use of a third party expert to settle certain specified matter, or disputes in general. There are several variations to this. There could be an expert to settle e.g. pricing matters, as in the old Iraq Petroleum Company Group Agreements which provided for an annual setting of a price by an expert at which oil would be sold to other shareholders. A third party expert can be requested to examine the situation and revise the contract if necessary, and it can be provided that his decision shall be binding on the parties. Alternatively the experts may be empowered only to make recommendations and not binding decisions.[1] If the parties do not agree to his recommendations the contract will continue in force as before. Again, provision can be made for a conciliator who will hear each parties side to the dispute and come up with a compromise that may or may not be binding on the two parties.
- Arbitration before a sole arbitrator or a panel of arbitrators in accordance with an agreed procedure.
- Litigation before a court located in the parties' choice of forum.

Within the oil industry, litigation is the option of last resort. When the other party is the government, the favoured option

[1] The second and third alternatives are included in a draft I.C.C. Hardship clause.

of the oil companies is usually renegotiation even when their legal rights have clearly been infringed. Third party dispute resolution with the government is generally avoided. The major exceptions to these were the oil nationalisation cases, and it is noteworthy that final settlements were the product of negotiation, and not of the award or judgement in question. Between the various categories of oil companies, e.g., between a producing company and a service company, arbitrations are often entered into and awards honoured.

Any contract should clearly provide for dispute settlement by arbitration or litigation. Normally, in an oil exploration and production contract, the clause will refer to arbitration, under domestic or international rules such as those of the International Centre for the Settlement of Investment Disputes (ICSID). Within Nigerian exploration and production contracts it is usually stipulated that the place of dispute settlement will be situated in Nigeria, and that the laws of Nigeria will be applicable. For arbitration, the governing law is the Arbitration and Conciliation Act 1988.

Selected reading materials

J. O. Orojo, M.A. Ajomo, *Law and Practice of Arbitration and Conciliation in Nigeria*, Mbeyi – Associates (Nigeria) Limited 1999 Particularly Chapters 4 and 5.

Y. Omorogbe, *op. cit.* pp. 104 –117.

Bibliography for further reading

General oil and gas texts

Lawrence Atsegbua, *Nigerian Petroleum Law - The Acquisition of Oil Rights in Nigeria*, L. A. Atsegbua, 1993.

G. Etikerentse, *Nigerian Petroleum Law*, Macmillan Publishers/London, 1985

M. M. Olisa, *Nigerian Petroleum Law and Practice*, 2nd Edn, 1997

Revision questions

Questions for the various topics

Topic 1

(1) What is petroleum?
(2) How is petroleum formed?
(3) How is it found?
(4) How is crude oil classified?
(5) What do the terms, 'sweet' and 'sour' crude oil means?
(6) Why is petroleum the world's most important commodity?
(7) What do you understand by the term energy? Describe it in your own words.
(8) "The physical state of petroleum is responsible for the peculiarities of the international oil and gas industry." Discuss.
(9) What are API degrees and what is their relationship to specific gravity?
(10) Why is it necessary to refine oil?
(11) "A major oil producing nation with poorly functioning

refineries is not much better off than an oil importing nation." Do you agree with this statement?

(12) Consider how your expertise as an oil and gas lawyer is enhanced by your understanding of the workings of the oil and gas industry.

Topic II

(13) Critically comment on the state of Nigerian legislation pertaining to the oil industry, with particular emphasis on the Petroleum Act 1969.

(14) Comment on the evolution of joint ventures in the Nigerian oil industry.

(15) Give a detailed description of the following rights:
- (i) oil exploration license
- (ii) oil prospecting license
- (iii) oil mining lease.

(16) Critically analyse the rights and powers of holders of OPLs and OMLs over the licensed or leased areas.

Topic III

(17) "In the United States, he who owns the land owns the oil and gas under it." Discuss.

(18) Critically assess the practical importance of ownership of a natural resource that a state lacks the capacity to control.

(19) Critically analyse the concept of ownership and consider the extent to which it can be regarded as an absolute right.

(20) What is the status of 'permanent sovereignty over natural resources' under international law?

Topic IV

(21) "The characteristics of the traditional concession were incapable of surviving decolonisation" and therefore, concessions no longer exist." Comment.
(22) Critically analyse the E and P contract that, in your view, is the most beneficial for the average developing host state.
(23) "The PSC has no benefits to offer to Nigeria." Do you agree with this sentence, which paraphrases the view of a tribunal which had cause to consider the merits and demerits of this type of contract? Is this view still prevalent in Nigeria today?
(24) "The Risk Service Contract is preferable to other E & P contracts." Do you agree with this view that was prevalent in Nigeria in the late '70s? Is this still the prevalent view? Give your answer, tracing the evolution of the RSC in Nigeria to date.
(25) Critically describe the various legal agreements that make up the joint venture relationship in the Nigerian oil and gas industry.
(26) Do you foresee pure service contracts and/or technical assistance agreements being utilised in Nigeria in the near future?
(27) Comment on Nigerian concession contracts, from inception to date.

Topic V

(28) In what ways is the international natural gas industry fundamentally different from that of crude oil?

(29) "Gas flaring is an environmentally harmful and wasteful practice'. Why?

(30) What are the problems of and prospects for the domestic utilisation of natural gas in Nigeria?

(31) With particular reference to the Nigeria LNG Limited assess the legal and practical efficacy of extensive guarantees and incentives, which even purport to bind the legislative arm of government indefinitely.

Topic VI

(32) Comment on the various sources of revenue derived from the oil industry by the Nigerian government.

(33) What are royalties and who are they payable to?

(34) Assess the incentives given by the Nigerian government to encourage natural gas investments.

(35) Describe the different stages necessary, m order to arrive at the correct figure for petroleum profits tax.

(36) What types of companies are engaged in petroleum operations?

Topic VII

(37) "OPEC is an organisation born of protest", Comment.

(38) Are the 'fundamentally similar interests' of OPEC members capable of definition?

(39) "If OPEC had not been created, oil and gas law in Nigeria, and in other developing states, would not be

what it is today"? Do you agree? Comment critically.

(40) Now that OPEC no longer controls oil prices, does it remain a viable organisation?

(41) Critically evaluate OPEC,
   (a) from a historical perspective
   (b) from a visionary perspective.

(42) What are the ways and means through which a state can cease to be a member of OPEC?

Topic VIII

(43) Why are national oil companies prevalent all over the world?

(44) Why have NOCs been less successful than their private counterparts?

(45) "The Act Establishing the NNIPC, and the NNPC as an entity have little or no resemblance" Comment.

(46) How and why did the NNPC evolve from the NNOC?

(47) What is the legal relationship, as contained within the necessary laws and within the Nigerian historical context, between NNPC and the Ministry of Petroleum Resources?

Topic IX

(48) Comment generally on the state of the downstream sector of the Nigerian oil industry.

(49) Does the law allow for third party access to pipeline grids?

(50) Advise a prospective company as to the state of refining in Nigeria, and how to become a refinery operator in Nigeria.

(51) Comment on Nigerian laws relating to the petrochemicals industry.

Topic X

(52) What or who controls the prices of crude oil?
(53) Advise an international crude oil trader as to how to become a buyer of Nigerian crude oil.
(54) "The spot market has no physical location. Nonetheless it is very real and vibrant." Expatiate on this statement.
(55) Critically analyse the workings of one spot market known to you.
(56) The average Nigerian comes into contact with the oil industry only when he buys petroleum products. The industry is assessed by the strengths or weakness of products trade and therefore, the average Nigerian would score less than average marks to this industry" Do you agree?

Topic XI

(57) What is the impact of international conventions on Nigerian environmental law?
(58) The oil industry is a major contributor to the world's environmental problems. How?
(59) Critically assess the adequacy and efficacy of Nigerian environmental law.
(60) How real are the threats posed to the world by climate change?
(61) Consider the problems and prospects associated with compliance with international environmental obligations by developing country oil producers such as Nigeria.

(62) Critically assess the OPEC position on climate change.

Topic XII

(63) To what extent do states, peoples and individuals have a right to development?
(64) Have communities any legal basis for asserting a right over any natural resources found beneath their land?
(65) Can indigenous people's rights be distinguished from local peoples rights?
(66) Read the Ogoni Bill of Rights and the Kaiama Declaration and assess their legal content and validity.
(67) In what ways can the law be strengthened so as to give adequate protection to persons and communities living in the oil producing areas?

Topic XIII

(68) Distinguish between the use of technology and the acquisition of technology.
(69) Analyse sections in the Petroleum Act 1969 which deal, directly or indirectly, with issues relating to technology transfer.
(70) Should indigenous participation in the oil industry be assisted and encouraged? Consider this, analysing pros and cons.
(71) (a) Trace the evolution of the 'Independents' in America.
(b) Trace the evolution of the Nigerian indigenous companies to date. Consider the similarities and dissimilarities.
(72) What is a marginal field?
(73) What, in your opinion, should be the national position on

marginal field allocation and production?

(74) Critically assess the successes and failures of:
(i) PTF
(ii) OMPADEC

(75) Is it necessary to make create special institutions such as the Petroleum Trust Fund and the Niger Delta Development Commission for the utilisation of oil revenues?

Topic XIV

(76) "The Niger Delta Development Commission Act is the product of compromise and politics rather than pragmatism" Comment.

(77) Distinguish between the traditional and emergent international laws on nationalisation?

(78) Why is participation referred to as 'creeping' nationalisation?

(79) To what extent has the Nigerian oil industry undergone privatisation so far?

(80) Is it feasible to expect that a critically important industry (such as the Nigerian oil and gas industry) can be successfully privatised?

(81) Why do nations privatise?

(82) Why do nations nationalise?

(83) The world has experienced a move from nationalisation to privatisation during the past decade. Could the reverse occur in the foreseeable future, in your opinion?

Topic XV

(84) Consider the arbitration clauses contained in oil and gas

agreements. Which form of dispute settlement is most prevalent?

(85) What factors militate against the use of litigation between companies and their host governments?

Index

www.ingramcontent.com/pod-product-compliance
Lightning Source LLC
Chambersburg PA
CBHW071442230926
51846CB00001B/312
9789780231330